Iowa Trout Streams

The Highweather Guide To

IOWA TROUT STREAMS

A Guide to the Streams and Rivers of Northeastern Iowa's Bluff Country

JENE HUGHES

THE HIGHWEATHER PRESS
SAINT PAUL, MINNESOTA

Copyright © 1994, 2000 by Jene Hughes

All rights reserved. No part of this work may be reproduced in part or in whole in any electronic or mechanical means including information storage and retrieval systems without permission in writing from the publisher.

The Highweather Press, LLC
Post Office Box 211314
Saint Paul, Minnesota 55121

The Highweather Press publishes fine regional fly-fishing guides. For a complete list, write to the address above.

ISBN 0-9632344-4-7

REVISED EDITION

10 9 8 7 6 5 4 3 2 1

Jacket maps are from the United States Geologic Survey, Highlandville and Decorah Quadrangles.

The publisher is grateful to the following individuals for their significant contributions to this project: Mike Lynch, Paul Mueller, Alan Spaulding, Brad Springer and Bob Trevis.

Maps by Brad Springer
Knot illustrations by Dave Schelitzche
Photographs on pages 68, 152, and back cover by author
Front cover and all other photographs by the publisher

The Highweather Press & Highweather Press logos are trademarks of The Highweather Press, LLC.
Book design copyright The Highweather Press

Dedication

To Mary,
who started this book decades ago
by allowing her ten-year-old son
to commandeer her fly rod.

Acknowledgments

When a voice from the lowest bunk rose out of the darkness to ask, "Hey Jene, wouldn't you like to live out here for a year and write a book about the streams?" I answered, "No, I'd like to take a year at home and write a book about *those* streams."

The voice belonged to Iowan Byron Haugh, who was putting me up in a friend's cabin on Idaho's Henry's Fork. A few weeks later I gave Byron an "assignment" to fish Bloody Run so we could compare notes as I worked on the manuscript for this project.

Accompanying me on that trip was Ron Fredrickson, my regular fishing buddy who first showed, and is still showing me, new spots and ways to fish the streams I call the Northern Triangle. Ron is the most enthusiastic fan of Iowa streams I know, and he blends a deadly color of Hare's Ear dubbing for the northern streams.

Pitching in with fishing information and suggestions was John Pursell, who started fly fishing at the first clinic I held in Iowa. He caught his first trout at Richmond Springs just a week or so after that clinic, and I think I was more pleased even than he.

Dave Moeller, who supervises fisheries in the DNR's Northeast Region, has always found time to answer my questions, as have many of his staff. The help they have given me is the merest reflection of their sincerity and genuine interest in trout and trout streams. Their work extends far beyond that of producing catchable fish, and we should all be grateful to them.

A large portion of what I know and am presenting here can, directly or indirectly, be traced back to a single angler: David Halblom. Dave, one of the founding members of the Hawkeye Fly Fishing Association, is a manufacturers' representative in the fly tackle industry, teaches fly tying at the Masters level, is active in the Federation of Fly Fishers (FFF) and even finds time to fish. When he does fish, it is with skill and precision that you rarely see on the streams. Any flaws or arguable points herein are definitely my doing, however, not the result of Dave's influence.

Finally, I wish to give special thanks to my wife Kathy. We have fished and worked together for many years, and her contributions to this project can only be described as enormous.

All of these people, along with countless visitors to my fly shop who are kind enough to report the results of their fishing excursions, have made it possible for me to gather enough information to assemble this book. I thank all of you.

CONTENTS

Acknowledgments...7
Publisher's Note..11
   Overall Map of Iowa Trout Streams................. 14-15
Preface to the Second Edition............................17

Part 1: Iowa Trout Fishing...............................21

   Iowa Trout Fishing...................................23

Part 2: The Trout Streams of Iowa 67

   Getting Around 69

   Protected Streams 75
      Spring Branch...............................77
      Ensign Hollow 83
      Bloody Run..................................86
      South Pine...................................89
      Upper and Lower French Creek 90

   The Northern Triangle 93
      Waterloo Creek 95
      North Bear Creek 98
      South Bear Creek 98
      French Creek................................102

   Decorah & The Upper Iowa River Basin 107
      Trout Run Creek 108
      Twin Springs 109
      Trout River and Coon Creek 110
      Patterson, Silver, and Pine Creeks 113
      West Canoe 116
      Coldwater Creek 118
      Bigalk Creek 120
      Bohemian Creek 122

   Along the Mississippi...............................123
      Clear Creek 124
      Wexford Creek 124

Iowa Trout Streams

```
Paint Creek ................................126
Little Paint Creek ..........................126
Hickory Creek .............................128
Sny Magill and North Cedar Creek ............130
Turkey River (Big Spring) ...................132
Buck Creek ...............................134
South Cedar ..............................136
```

Fayette County 137
```
Otter and Glovers Creeks .....................138
Grannis and Bear Creeks .....................140
Mink Creek ...............................142
```

The Backbone Area & East 143
```
Richmond Springs .........................143
Joy Springs and Maquoketa River ..............146
Little Turkey River .........................146
Fountain Springs and Twin Bridges ............148
Bankston .................................150
```

Swiss Valley & The Southern Streams 153
```
Upper and Lower Swiss Valley (Catfish Creek) ...154
Big Mill Creek .............................156
Little Mill Creek ...........................159
Brush Creek ..............................161
```

The Trout Country Panhandle 163
```
Spring Creek ..............................164
Turtle Creek ..............................165
Wapsi (Wapsipinicon) River ..................166
```

Part 3: Reflections 169
In Retrospect 171
Loose Ends 175
```
The Improved Clinch Knot ...................177
The Perfection Loop ........................178
The Double Surgeon's Knot ..................180
```

Index of Streams 185
Appendix 189

Publisher's Note

More than a decade ago, I made a brief business trip to northeastern Iowa. I did not take my fishing gear. Like most Americans, I held an image of Iowa as a vast, flat checkerboard of fertile farmland. It seemed hardly the place to find trout fishing.

My trip took me through Winneshiek and Allamakee counties, into what I now know is the heart of Iowa's trout region. Through lovely small towns, down winding two-

Iowa Trout Streams

lane blacktop and over dusty gravel roads, with each succeeding mile I was charmed. I discovered an unexpected landscape of deep valleys, high limestone bluffs, old forests and rushing trout streams.

Why had I assumed that Iowa lacked trout? Perhaps it was the same reason so few people are aware that there are trout streams *anywhere* in the Midwest. It is "flyover" country. At that time, few people talked about Iowa's trout streams, fewer wrote about them in the popular fly-fishing magazines.

All that changed in 1994, when Jene Hughes, the irrepressible owner of a bait and fly shop in Des Moines, wrote and self-published the first edition of *Iowa Trout Streams*, the first serious guide to trout fishing in Iowa. Suddenly, the world learned of Iowa's spring creeks.

Jene's book shattered the myth that Iowa was a broad featureless agricultural state. In fact, to read Jene's book, one might get the impression that Iowa is rugged and hilly and peppered with trout streams from the Mississippi River clear to Nebraska. In reality, Iowa's trout region is tucked away in a small corner of the state. It is a part of the larger "Driftless Area," a geologically unique vestige of the last ice age. The Driftless Area is an area of rugged uplands covering portions of Iowa, Wisconsin, Minnesota and Illinois untouched by the glaciers. It is beautiful country, a world apart from the Great Plains so close at hand. It's a region of clear, rushing limestone spring creeks and, of course, trout.

In the fall of 1997, Highweather Press acquired the rights to Jene's book and convinced him to write a new edition. On a cold October day, I met with Jene and his wife, Kathy, to sign the paperwork over a cup of coffee at the Sportsmen Motel and Cafe near Dorchester, Iowa. The conversation meandered like nearby Waterloo Creek, from trout fishing to horse racing to bluegrass music. Jene's unbridled passion for life was—and is—contagious.

I'm delighted that Jene's book is now part of the Highweather Press, and pleased that he has written this thoroughly revised and updated edition. I know it will continue to cast new light on this beautiful, overlooked corner of Iowa, and the excellent trout fishing this area has to offer. I hope you take the time to explore this region. I know you will fall in love—as I have—with these streams.

John van Vliet
June, 2000

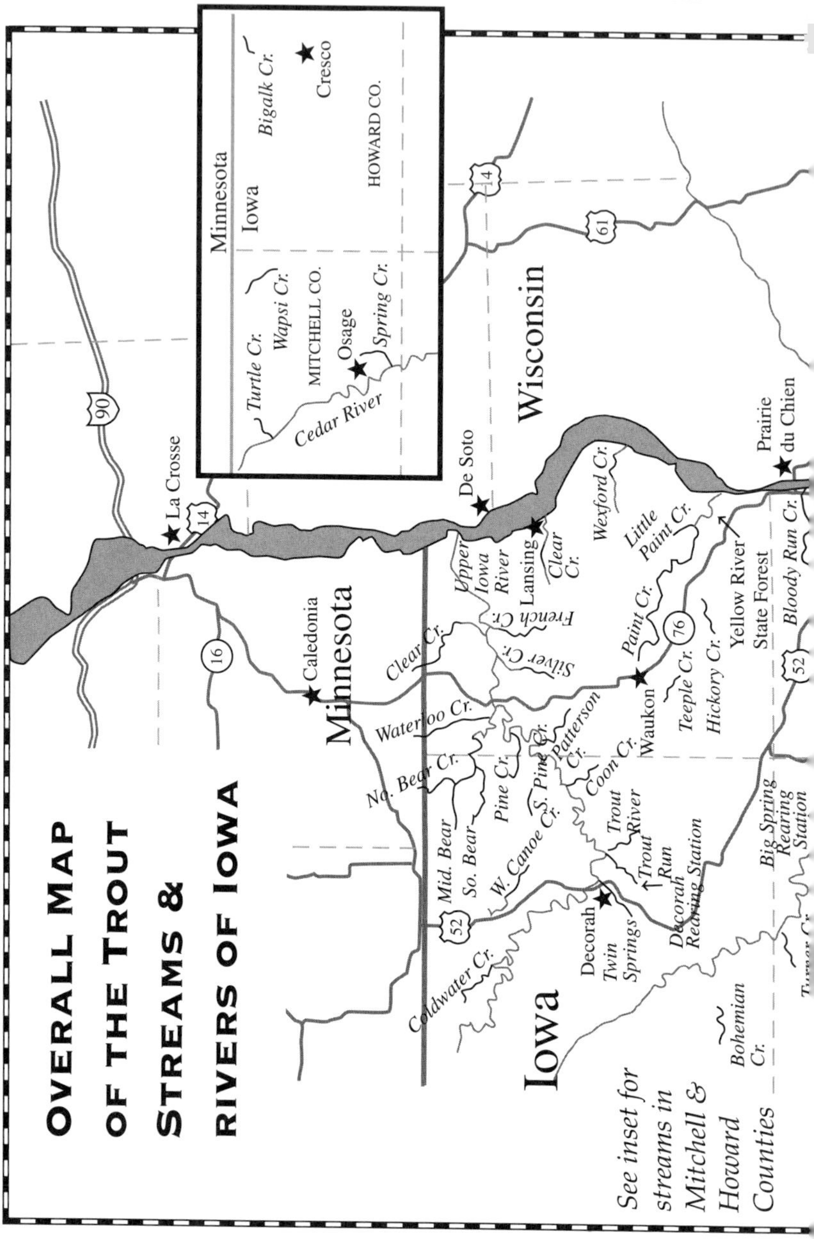

Iowa Trout Streams

OVERALL MAP OF THE TROUT STREAMS & RIVERS OF IOWA

See inset for streams in Mitchell & Howard Counties

Inset (Mitchell & Howard Counties, Minnesota/Iowa border):
- Minnesota / Iowa
- Bigalk Cr.
- ★ Cresco
- HOWARD CO.
- Turtle Cr.
- Wapsi Cr.
- MITCHELL CO.
- Osage ★
- Spring Cr.
- Cedar River

Main map labels:
- Minnesota, Wisconsin, Iowa
- La Crosse ★ (US 90, US 14)
- Caledonia ★
- De Soto ★
- Prairie du Chien ★
- Lansing ★
- Waukon ★
- Decorah ★
- US 61, Hwy 16, Hwy 14, Hwy 52, Hwy 76

Streams:
- Clear Cr.
- Upper Iowa River
- French Cr.
- Silver Cr.
- Clear Cr.
- Wexford Cr.
- Little Paint Cr.
- Paint Cr.
- Yellow River State Forest
- Bloody Run Cr.
- Waterloo Cr.
- No. Bear Cr.
- Mid. Bear Cr.
- So. Bear Cr.
- Pine Cr.
- S. Pine Cr.
- W. Canoe Cr.
- Patterson Cr.
- Coon Cr.
- Teeple Cr.
- Hickory Cr.
- Trout River
- Trout Run
- Decorah Rearing Station
- Big Spring Rearing Station
- Coldwater Cr.
- Twin Springs
- Bohemian Cr.
- Turkey Cr.

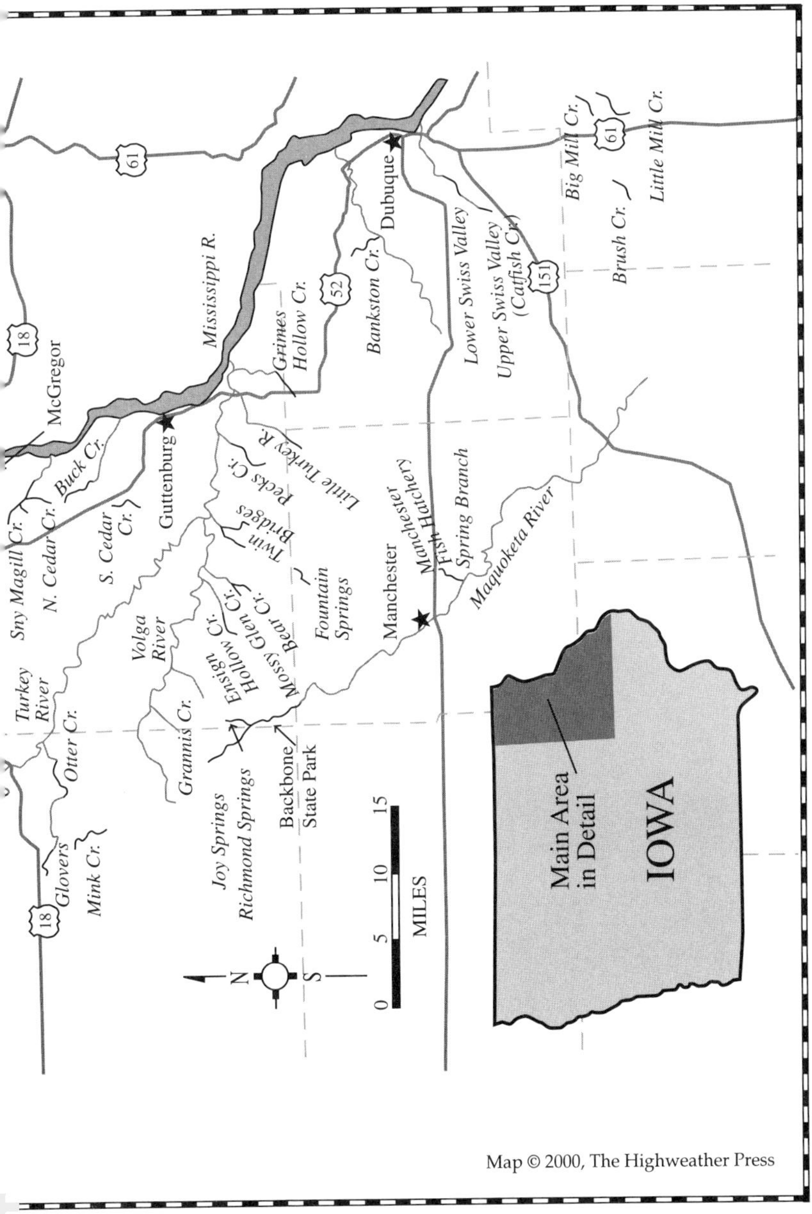
Mississippi R.
McGregor
Guttenburg
Dubuque
Manchester
Sny Magill Cr.
N. Cedar Cr.
Buck Cr.
S. Cedar Cr.
Turkey River
Otter Cr.
Glovers
Mink Cr.
Volga River
Grannis Cr.
Joy Springs
Richmond Springs
Ensign Hollow Cr.
Glen Cr.
Mossy Bear Cr.
Backbone State Park
Twin Bridges
Pecks Cr.
Little Turkey R.
Grimes Hollow Cr.
Fountain Springs
Bankston Cr.
Manchester Fish Hatchery
Spring Branch
Maquoketa River
Lower Swiss Valley
Upper Swiss Valley (Catfish Cr.)
Big Mill Cr.
Brush Cr.
Little Mill Cr.
18
61
52
151
N
S
0
5
10
15
MILES
Main Area in Detail
IOWA

Preface to the
Second Edition

A little more than six years have passed since the first edition of *Iowa Trout Streams* was published. When I signed the first printed copies for my friends in the fly-tying class at our shop, scarcely ten weeks had elapsed from the time I typed the first paragraph. Most of those ten weeks I'd spent in northeastern Iowa, driving the back roads and fishing. At that time I felt a sense of urgency to get accurate, useful information into the hands of the growing number of new fly anglers who were seeking advice on where to go and how to fish in Iowa.

Now, six years (and one Jeep) later, I have filled in the gaps and made this new edition of the book truly comprehensive. With the exception of the "put-and-grow" streams, for which you must obtain specific landowner permission to

Iowa Trout Streams

fish, every trout stream in Iowa is discussed here. Of the streams new to this edition, several are important ones that, for one reason or another, were omitted from the first edition. Others can be regarded as "side trips"—decent places to fish, but perhaps too small to warrant a full day's attention. And then there are a few streams, surprisingly few, included here only for the sake of completeness.

My philosophy regarding the significance of any given stream is that every stream has at least one redeeming quality, if only the simple fact that it's there. If you happen to be there too, that makes two redeeming qualities. In other words, discriminating taste in trout streams doesn't necessarily lead to more enjoyable fishing, and it can lead, unhappily, to less fishing. There isn't a stream discussed in these pages that I would deliberately avoid.

Along with adding new stream listings, I have in several places rearranged the original material, elaborated on some of the initial advice I offered, and added new material where I thought it would be helpful.

Those are most of the changes to the content of the book. (Of course we've changed the design of the book, too.) As for the streams, and Iowa trout fishing itself, the changes over the last six years have been, in general, for the better. Though nature and state agencies move slowly, there have been some obvious improvements. For example, though there was a general awareness of wild browns in French Creek when we went to press six years ago, there had been little if any public mention of them. Only after careful study did the DNR announce their documentation of wild browns and subsequently propose special regulations on the stream. The support that the proposal received is an indication of the increased awareness and appreciation of stream-born trout in Iowa. Recent news releases concerning Waterloo Creek have been quick to point out the naturally reproducing fish there. While most of the state's streams will continue to depend on stocking, or at least be enhanced by it, the current interest in identifying and protecting those streams that can support wild trout populations is a welcome change.

The presence of stream-born trout is also an indication that recent efforts at improving agricultural practices are paying off. "Protecting" natural populations of fish is, I would guess, as much or more an environmental issue as it is a matter of regulating angling and stocking practices. All in all, six years have brought cleaner water, larger populations of wild fish, and greater public access to trout waters.

—JDH
May, 2000

PART 1

IOWA TROUT FISHING

A popular stretch of challenging water on Iowa's Spring Branch Creek.

Iowa Trout Fishing

My first trout fishing trip to northeast Iowa was, to put it mildly, a disappointment. Years had passed since I had last visited that corner of the state, and the only publication showing the location of the trout streams was a poorly printed map derived from the state's official transportation map. Finding the streams was frustrating, and when I finally managed to locate a couple of them, I found that these clear spring creeks presented a unique set of challenges. By the time I got back to Des Moines, I wasn't sure I had once cast a fly over a trout. In fact I wasn't even sure where I'd been most of the time.

My purpose in these pages is to help new fly anglers—as well as experienced anglers new to Iowa—avoid some of the trail blazing I have done. The information in these pages is my attempt to see that fly anglers get off to a good start on these beautiful streams.

For that reason, I am including as much general fly-fishing information as I think might be useful, even though there is an abundance of fly-fishing advice available in other books. If you're an experienced fly angler, you can skip over some of the more basic information, but perhaps my suggestions will give you a new perspective that can improve your chances of success on the streams of Iowa, and elsewhere.

You may notice that the map of Spring Branch Creek is

different from the other maps in this book. I have annotated it in detail to give beginning fly anglers the help they may need to find fish and be successful quickly. This stream is so widely known that there are no "secret spots," and even if there were, the regulations protecting the stream reassure me that divulging the good holes won't fill someone's freezer at the expense of quality sport fishing for others.

All of the other maps are included simply to show you how to get to the streams and find fishable water with a minimum of frustration. The few fishing spots indicated are the more visible, already popular holes. If you are reading this book to learn "hot spots," you will be disappointed. The maps are solely to help you get your feet on the ground (or, rather, in the water). Learning the streams is up to you, and is one of the true joys of Iowa fishing. Fishing and exploring on your own will lead you to finding favorite areas that are scarcely treated here. As with many trout-fishing regions, ninety percent of Iowa trout fishing is done on ten percent of the water, or less.

I saw a poster once for a motorcycle club rally that held a sage piece of advice: "Leave your attitudes at home." That sentiment could be expressed in more refined prose, but it could not be more true. If you set out with reservations about the quality of Iowa trout fishing, you will probably confirm them on the streams. This book is for those who can appreciate the magic of small-stream fishing.

TROUT IN IOWA

When I asked my son Jesse what he would like to see in this book, he said this: "Reassure the readers that there are actually big fish in the streams." He held his hands about 14 inches apart and said, "Not just nice fish, but," and he moved his hands to 24 inches apart, "*nice* fish."

And that's true. But to fully enjoy Iowa trout fishing

Iowa Trout Streams

you must also enjoy the challenge of hooking and landing fish in the 10-inch to 15-inch range in small streams that are difficult to read and a challenge to your casting technique. It is by building on that experience that you will find the larger fish that indeed are there.

Prerequisite to getting the feel of Iowa trout fishing and the streams is studying the official map published by the Department of Natural Resources. It is your source of current information on how various streams are managed and stocked, and which waters are protected by special regulations. Don't be put off by the notion that stocked fish are imbeciles that will rise to anything. As you will see, that is simply not true. I can think of only a couple of states with trout fishing, even the states renowned for it, that don't have a stocking program of one sort or another.

The state trout maps are not always available at the stores that sell fishing licenses and trout stamps. If your travels take you near the hatchery, or one of the rearing stations, you can get a copy there. They are also available at the offices of some of the state parks in trout country. To request one by mail, contact:

>Iowa Department of Natural Resources
>Wallace State Office Building
>Des Moines, Iowa 50319-0034
>Telephone 515-281-5145

Iowa's Fisheries

The trout management program in Iowa divides trout fisheries into three categories: Catchable, Put-and-grow and Special. Catchable fisheries, informally referred to as "put-and-take" streams, encompass most of Iowa's trout water. The second category, put-and-grow fisheries, is comprised of streams that are less accessible to the public. The third category, special fisheries, consists primarily of streams that carry special regulations. (Special fisheries also include three small urban lakes that are stocked only as winter trout fisheries, and will not be discussed in this book.)

In some instances, the special and catchable designations overlap. For example, Bloody Run has both catchable and special sections, while French Creek, though designated as special because the brown trout there are protected, is nevertheless stocked with catchable rainbow trout.

Because the regulations governing the special fisheries make them especially appealing to fly anglers, they are the first ones discussed in Part 2 of this book. The following sections of this chapter provide a general description of the catchable and put-and-grow streams.

Catchable (Put-and-Take) Streams

These streams make up the majority of Iowa's trout waters and are the most popular fisheries. Put-and-take streams are stocked regularly with catchable-size trout reared at one of Iowa's three rearing stations. The stocked trout range in size from 10 to 12 inches. Depending on the stream, stocking is announced either before or after it takes place. In either event, anglers often flock to recently stocked streams.

In spite of the tremendous numbers of rainbow trout stocked by the state, Iowa trout fishing at its best is generally brown-trout fishing, and to experience it at its best you must learn to work within the Department of Natural Resources' extensive put-and-take program that stocks 360,000 catchable fish annually. The best way to merge quality fly fishing with the established program is to ignore the stocking trucks, or better still, make every attempt to avoid them. In the wake of the stocking truck come crowds of anglers whose preference is for treble hooks baited with Velveeta cheese. Avoid them, but don't cuss them. It's the trout that elude them and leave the stocking holes to take

Iowa Trout Streams

up residence elsewhere in the stream that give fly anglers their sport fishing. I think of these as "resident" fish, but they are generally called "hold-overs" or "carry-overs." From them have arisen populations of wild, stream-born browns.

Of the three stocked species—brown, rainbow, and brook trout—it is the browns that provide the best sport fishing for fly anglers. Generally rainbows do not survive as well in Iowa streams as the browns, and because of their kinship to steelheads they have a greater tendency to migrate downstream, especially in the autumn. This migratory tendency diminished significantly with the introduction of the Shasta strain of rainbows, but anglers may still encounter good rainbow fishing a considerable distance below the portion of a stream that is designated as "trout waters."

When those of us who release most of our fish want a couple of fish for supper, it is the rainbows we keep. They make up about 75% of the stocking. On the other hand, brown trout are the hardiest of the group and survive well in Iowa waterways, so each individual caught should be handled carefully and released immediately. Before tying on a fly, pinch down the barb or, when you can, use barbless hooks. Resident brown trout are your opportunity for a 20-inch fish someday.

Brook trout, originally native to Iowa, do well in our streams and are lovely fish and fun to catch. They simply don't achieve the size of the browns. The stocking of brook trout is relatively limited (about 5% of the stocking total), but in 1992 the state launched a put-and-grow program in a limited number of streams. One protected stream, South Pine, has a self-sustaining population of wild brook trout that many people believe are the descendants of the fish found in Iowa in pioneer times. Genetic testing has shown that this strain of fish is not related to any that the DNR has ever used for stocking. Specimens of this population have been relocated to other waters to promote its survival. There are a couple of other small streams that might hold wild brookies from the Ice Age, but the likelihood is that if you catch a brook trout, it has been stocked.

For purposes of size comparison, disregard Iowa's published record of big fish. The record-holding fish are hatchery brood trout that have been moved into the streams, generally to be caught within a day or two of release. To me, considering that I customarily use dry flies and comparatively light tackle, a good day of fishing is one in which I catch several (or more) fish in the 12-inch class and one or two in the 15-inch class. In general, you can apply the same size criterion to Iowa fish as to those anywhere else: a 20-inch fish, particularly one caught on a #20 fly, is more than sufficient excuse to drag out the camera.

PUT-AND-GROW STREAMS

As the name implies, these streams are stocked with fingerlings to produce stream-raised trout rather than ones grown to catchable size in rearing stations. The streams classified as put-and-grow streams are stocked only once a year and have an immense appeal, though they rarely meet our expectations. That is not to say they don't have fish or merit, but that for the journeying angler they will more often than not lead to disappointment. They lend themselves well to hiking and exploring, and for the angler with ample time, some of them might indeed produce excellent results. But the time spent seeking permission and access to the streams, and then looking for fish in them, often exceeds the time spent fishing. As a result, you should save the put-and-grow streams for when you build your retirement cabin in the region, or allow time for exploring one at the end of your trip—after you have had some rewarding fishing on the put-and-take water.

When you do decide to check out these streams, spend plenty of advance time with your maps. On the DNR map,

PUT-AND-GROW STREAMS

Stream Name	County	Nearest Town
Clear	Allamakee	Dorchester
Erickson Branch	Allamakee	Lansing
Teeple	Allamakee	Waukon
Bear	Clayton	Edgewood
Mossy Glen	Clayton	Strawberry Point
Pecks	Clayton	Osterdock
West Fk. Sny Magill	Clayton	McGregor
Grimes Hollow*	Delaware	Colesburg
Ram Hollow*	Delaware	Colesburg
Spring Falls	Delaware	Colesburg
Hogan's Branch	Dubuque	Epworth
Little Maquoketa	Dubuque	Epworth
Turner	Fayette	St. Lucas
Beaver	Howard	Lime Springs
Staff	Howard	Chester
Pleasant	Jackson	Springbrook
South Fk. Big Mill	Jackson	Bellevue
Burr Oak	Mitchell	Brownville
Rock	Mitchell	Osage
Casey Springs	Winneshiek	Decorah
East Pine	Winneshiek	Bluffton
Middle Bear*	Winneshiek	Highlandville
North Canoe*	Winneshiek	Locust
Pine	Winneshiek	Bluffton
Ten Mile*	Winneshiek	Decorah

*Experimental brook trout stocking

stream locations are described by the Township, Range, and Section. Township numbers appear up and down the sides of these maps to indicate horizontal lines, and Range numbers indicate their vertical counterparts, with the numbers appearing across the top or bottom. At the intersection of Township and Range lines you will find the small numbered squares that are the Sections through which the stream flows.

If you have time and enjoy armchair exploring, there is great potential here, particularly if you use detailed maps. If you don't want to buy the numerous detailed topographical maps, consider getting county topographical maps, which will give you additional help finding the put-and-take streams.

Let me add a note of caution here: If you find a good put-and-grow stream, remember that any fish removed from it will take years to replace. These streams are not stocked with catchable fish. You also should think twice about sharing your information with anyone.

Iowa Trout Streams

Tight quarters demand skill, but often produce large trout.

Having the right equipment and knowing how to use it are the keys to catching trout.

CHOOSING THE RIGHT TACKLE

I'm frequently asked what type of tackle I recommend for fishing Iowa's streams. Below are some guidelines and my personal recommendations. Ultimately, your choice of gear must be based on a number of factors, including your casting ability, personal preferences, time available for small-stream fishing, and most importantly, the number of rods you own or hope to own.

Rods

At the outset, I'll answer the question I am most often asked: For Iowa's streams, I recommend a 7- to 8-foot rod for a 4-weight line.

I usually carry three short, light rods—one each in 2-, 3-, and 4-weight. The 2-weight is for extremely small flies in still, clear water, while the 4-weight is for hopper patterns or windy days. Were I limited to a single rod, I would choose a 7-foot 4-weight. I use and endorse 3-piece rods, which are convenient and cast as well (or better) than their 2-piece counterparts.

If you are just starting out, here is a selection of three rods that for an Iowa angler will cover most situations:

7' for #4	Small streams everywhere
9' for #6	Lakes and ponds, especially from a canoe or float tube; Western trout; smallmouth
9' for #8	Largemouth bass; pike; steelhead; light saltwater; stripers in Iowa's larger tailwaters

The frequent presence of brush and overhanging branches is only one reason for using short rods. With a short rod it is much easier to produce casts that are short yet nonetheless straighten out low over the water. Imagine that the water between you and a fish is the base of a triangle, while your rod pointing skyward is a second side. The line from the rod tip reaches the fish and completes the triangle, and the longer the rod is, the sharper the downward angle will be. With a shorter rod the line is more parallel to the water. Kneeling along the stream, in addition to diminishing your silhouette, lowers the rod tip even more.

A shorter rod is simply easier to cast well at close range and in close quarters, especially when a delicate presentation is needed.

Iowa Trout Streams

FLY LINES

The two primary fly-line tapers to consider for fishing the small streams of Iowa are weight-forward (WF) and double-taper (DT).

Weight-forward lines are designed with most of their weight in the first 30 feet (roughly one-third of the line's overall length), tapering to a thinner section, called *running line*, which makes up the remainder of the line. This concentration of weight at the front end makes these lines superior for casting greater distances, punching flies into the wind, or throwing heavier flies.

Double-taper lines have a long, uniformly thick midsection, called the *belly*, with identical tapers at each end of the line. They cast well at short to medium distances and in some situations they perform better than weight-forward lines because they don't have the transition to running line at 30 feet that can cause a weight-forward line to "hinge." Perhaps the greatest advantage of double-tapers is that they are essentially two fly lines in one: if the line wears out or is damaged at one end, you can simply turn it around rather than replace it.

Since most small-stream fishing requires relatively short casts, the difference between double taper and weight forward is negligible. Weight-forward line will enable you to shoot more line on casts over 30 feet, but once on the water it is difficult to mend or roll cast because the slender "running" portion is on the water between you and the weight-forward "head" of the line.

It is rare that you will have the full 30-foot head of a weight forward line out of the rod tip on an Iowa stream. For this reason, steer away from "triangle taper" lines and those promoted as "spring creek" lines. These lines have very long, gradual front tapers that, in my experience, fail to load most rods sufficiently at close range.

At least one brand of line comes in a choice of harder or softer coating. The harder-coated lines cast better because

35

they slip through the guides more easily and sag less between the guides. The softer-coated lines are more flexible and bend easily to drift naturally in the slow currents you often encounter on Iowa streams. I recommend the softer line.

Another factor to consider in choosing a line is buoyancy. Today's fly lines are designed to float high on the water or sink at a specific rate. While sinking lines have their uses, stick with floating lines for fishing Iowa.

The last factor in choosing a fly line is color. The most popular colors of fly line are light or fluorescent. While these colors are easy for the angler to see in the air and on the water, some people feel they can spook the fish. But, in most cases, the long leader is sufficient to keep the tip of the fly line out of the fish's vision, making fly-line color largely a matter of personal preference.

LEADERS & TIPPETS

Even more than fly-line tapers and weights, leaders demand careful attention. They are the critical link between your line and your fly, ultimately determining the success of each cast and thus your overall fishing success.

The connection between fly line and fly is one of the most overlooked factors in fly fishing. A good leader not only forms a transparent link between fly line and fly, it also helps transfer the energy of the cast smoothly and efficiently, and it allows the fly to drift naturally in the current.

When you remove a new "knotless" leader from its package, the tippet (the fine end where you attach the fly) is part of the unit. If you are using the typical 9-foot, 6X trout leader, you should carry a spool of 6X tippet material to replace the tippet you lose by changing flies. The "X" designation represents thousandths of an inch in diameter, with 0X equaling .011, 1X equaling .010, and so forth.

Iowa Trout Streams

Standard procedure is to carry an assortment of tippet material so leaders can be customized to changing fishing conditions. For example, when fishing smooth, slow water you need fine tippet, usually 6X or even 7X, that will allow your flies to drift naturally on the surface. (We call it "drag" when the leader or current causes your fly to drift unnaturally.) Envision the trout in the stream, facing into the current, watching the movable feast passing over its head. It is essential that your fly drifts just like the cottonwood seed, the piece of bark, and the real insects that are floating along with it.

Using small flies and fine tippet, such as a #18 fly with 6X tippet, is typical in slow water. Should you need to go below a size 20 fly, you will probably want to use 7X tippet. A common solution to the problem of finicky fish, especially in heavily fished catch-and-release streams, is to try smaller and smaller flies. In my experience, the fish are less wary of the fly than they are the leader, that is to say, they are "leader shy." Before resorting to extremely small flies and 8X tippet, try using one of the brands of fluorocarbon tippet material (Cortland's Climax and Orvis's Mirage come to mind). You might not need it all of the time, but I am convinced that in some situations it works wonders.

In faster, rippled water it is typical to use larger flies that are more visible to both you and the fish. This calls for a heavier tippet that has the strength to "turn the fly over" so the cast straightens out completely. Heavier tippet is also valuable when the wind comes up. Many of us are guilty of not changing tippet size as we make changes in fly size, and it costs us fish. A 4X leader might be too heavy for most situations, but you'll definitely need one in August to cast your hopper patterns with accuracy and authority.

In addition to the size of tippet material, be aware that individual brands vary in stiffness and their resulting ability to turn over a fly at the end of the cast. When selecting tippet material and leaders, notice that for any given size, the breaking weights are different for different brands of material. Those with the higher test strength are actually softer and will drift more naturally in a slow current and stretch more before breaking, but they will not turn the fly over as well as their lower test, stiffer counterparts. Harder material is also more resistant to abrasion.

For nymph fishing you might consider a 7' 6" leader and add to it another foot or so of tippet; the resulting knot will keep your split shot from sliding down to the fly.

Common practice is to install a "permanent leader butt" on the fly line so leaders can be replaced without cutting away any of the fly line's tip. A permanent leader butt consists of three or four inches of heavy monofilament permanently attached to the end of your fly line, with a small loop (preferably a Perfection Loop, page 178) which in turn mates with a similar loop tied at the end of the leader's butt section. If the permanent butt is fashioned from brightly colored monofilament, it doubles as a "strike indicator" to watch when fishing nymphs or other flies below the surface.

Many anglers have found that tying their own complete leaders from varying sizes of monofilament increases their ability to turn over the fly. Hand tied leaders are also available commercially. I recommend that you carry a generous supply of leaders and, rather than discarding them, rebuild them in the comfort of your home. It's a shame to throw away a leader just because you have "nibbled" too far up into the taper.

For the small, clear streams of Iowa, the longer and finer the leader the better. Experienced anglers sometimes snip off a foot or so of the tip of a new leader and add a couple of feet of additional tippet material, thus increasing the overall length of the tippet. Give plenty of thought to your leader, and experiment with several different brands.

Iowa Trout Streams

REELS

Select a reel that is designed for the rod and line weight you're using. A single-action, ratchet-and-pawl reel is sufficient for landing most fish. A reel must have a drag of some sort to prevent over-spooling as you, or a fish, strip line from the reel.

I advise most beginners to concentrate on selecting a good rod and line first and then to chose their reel, bearing in mind that weight is a key factor in the design of the more expensive, high-performance rods; be careful not to sabotage your investment in a rod by being overly frugal in selecting a reel.

Many anglers are either attracted to or put off by the sound of a given reel. One that has an annoying sound to you in the shop will indeed wear on your nerves on a quiet stream.

The better reels are machined to very close tolerances, which gives smoother performance and increases resistance to dirt, gravel, and "icing up" in the winter.

WADING GEAR

One of the most often asked questions from anglers who have never fished Iowa is: "What kind of waders do I need?"

Your choice of wading gear depends mainly on the depth and temperature of the water.

My very strong opinion is that medium or light weight chest waders will contribute to your success nearly as much as a good rod, maybe more. The height will allow you to negotiate passage through deeper water to get around logs and rocks, and it will also permit you to kneel in the stream to make a strategic cast. Wading shoes or boots with felt soles will give you sure footing on most types of stream bottoms. Chest waders give you access to more water, but can be hot and uncomfortable to walk in for long distances.

For streams that you know to be shallow, lightweight "hippers" are good auxiliary wading gear. In place of expensive waders, I recommend buying modestly priced waders and spending the savings to supplement them with lightweight hippers and possibly summer-weight chest waders.

Another good compromise is the breathable chest- or waist-high wader, which uses Gore-Tex, or a similar material, to allow perspiration to escape while keeping you dry. Their single disadvantage is their cost, which can be prohibitively high.

If you plan to walk much, opt for stockingfoot wading gear so you get the ankle support provided by the separate boots with laces. This combination also gives you the option of wading wet, that is, wearing the shoes with neoprene socks and skipping the waders altogether.

NETS AND AIDS FOR RELEASING FISH

Although many anglers fish without a net, I am convinced that a long, shallow "catch-and-release" net is easier on a fish because you can play it less, land it sooner, and at least partially avoid squeezing it in your hand to bring it under control.

When you catch a trout, turning it over on its back will subdue it dramatically, and it will remain practically motionless while you remove the hook. Although most anglers still use a hemostat, or forceps, to remove hooks, many guides now use a release tool called the "Ketchum Release," which eliminates the need to touch the fish at all.

When the hook is visible you can often slide your hand down the leader, grip the fly, and unhook the fish underwater without touching it.

If you do have to hold the fish, moisten your hand first to avoid disturbing or removing the fish's protective slime.

Gadgets, Accessories and Floatant

In addition to the rod, reel, line and leader, you'll need a few other essentials to help make your fishing easier and more successful. These include fly floatant, a split-shot assortment, strike indicators, nippers to cut and trim the leader, and a hemostat, which in addition to freeing badly hooked fish, is handy for pinching down the barb of your hook. I've also used mine to release a badly hooked angler.

When it comes to keeping the fly afloat, I have come to rely on a combination of things that are worth mentioning here. First is the standard floatant you use when you first tie on the dry fly. A squirt or two from a pump or aerosol container is enough (some brands may change the color of the fly if you use too much). An alternative is the more economical paste that you apply with your fingers. Yet another type is a liquid that evaporates quickly and leaves a fine film of paraffin on the fly you have dipped into it.

After you've caught a fish on one of your flies, you're often faced with the problem of re-floating that fly. Not only is it soaked, it's slimy. My procedure for restoring the fly takes far less than a minute and includes using an Amadou, which in my opinion is one of nature's truly remarkable creations. An amadou, called "the mushroom" by some fly fishermen, is exactly that—two thin slices of a species of mushroom that absorbs water at a rate that puts the average sponge to shame. The slices are set in two pieces of leather. You simply press the fly gently between the two pieces of amadou, and the mushroom absorbs the water from the fly.

Here's the routine for re-floating a fly: First, I shake the fly briskly underwater to clean it off and revive the smashed hackle. Next, I squeeze it dry with the amadou. Then I shake it in the container of desiccant crystals and blow on the fly to remove excess dust and powder. Last, I apply the same floatant as when I began. Once you get accustomed to having these things stowed handily in your vest, the whole process becomes automatic and the fly is as good as new.

Additional useful items will usually work their way onto your "necessities" list. They include a Ty-Rite tool, on which I personally rely heavily for helping me hold small flies without smashing them; some type of pocket light; and a magnifier.

As you become more and more familiar with the insect life of the streams, a small seine is valuable. Some anglers also carry a thermometer.

To satisfy curiosity and keep yourself honest, wrap a piece of tape around your rod at a measured distance as an alternative to carrying a measuring tape.

An angler working the "improved" section of Spring Branch near the Manchester Hatchery.

NATURALS & ARTIFICIALS

Trout in streams rely on the current to provide a steady supply of aquatic insects and other foods, such as minnows, leeches and crustaceans, as well as terrestrial insects. Of these foods, aquatic insects make up the largest portion of a trout's diet. The four main groups of aquatic insects include mayflies, caddisflies, stoneflies and midges. Though "hatches," the emergence of the adult forms of aquatic insects, occur only sporadically (though fairly predictably) throughout the season, the immature forms of these insects (larvae, pupae and nymphs) are present all year long. These immature forms make up as much as ninety percent of a trout's diet. And though trout often feed opportunistically, it's their tendency to feed selectively that has earned them their reputation as an "intelligent" gamefish.

When trout are feeding selectively, such as during a heavy insect hatch, it's important to have a fly pattern that closely imitates the particular stage, size, shape, color and action of the natural. The hatch charts that follow do not include every individual species of insect found in the streams of the Iowa; rather, they are designed to help you identify which insects you're likely to encounter throughout the season, and which fly pattern best imitates a particular insect. Conversely, not all the aquatic insects listed on the hatch charts are present in all streams, but these charts should give you a fairly good idea which patterns to stock up on before you go.

When you encounter an insect hatch of any sort, match size first, then color. Identifying the insects will come later, or it won't, depending on the extent of your interest in insects; it is not essential to catching fish. I once fished with a Colorado guide who dipped his seine in the water and gathered a specimen that he held up and scrutinized carefully before proclaiming, "Well, it's about a size 18, and it's kinda cream colored."

In his fly box we found something about the right size and color and he tied it on my leader. Within seconds I hooked a trophy fish.

The easiest way to start learning insects is by fishing with someone who can teach you. Ron Fredrickson and I once climbed a mountain of firewood that was stacked against the side of a roadhouse so he could show me the Tricos that were swarming around the neon Budweiser sign in the window. The next morning, as Ron had predicted, there was a great Trico spinner fall, early, before the other hatches started coming off. It's hard to believe that huge trout will take something so small, but they will if it drifts over in such a way that the trout don't have to move.

You should at least learn enough about insects to distinguish caddisflies from mayflies. The flies listed on page 52 are ones I consider essential, and I carry at least two or three of each size at all times.

MAYFLIES (Ephemeroptera)

Species	Common Name or Imitation	Size	April	May	June	July	August	Sept.
Baetis vagans, intercalaris, others	Blue-wing Olive (BWO) Tiny BWO	16-22	■	■			■	■
Ephemerella subvaria	Dark Hendrickson	12-14		■				
Paraleptophlebia adoptiva & mollis	Blue Quill Blue Dun	16-18		■	■			
Ephemerella invaria & rotunda	Light Hendrickson Sulphur Duns	14-16		■	■			
Stenonema vicarium & fuscum	March Brown Gray Fox	10-16			■	■		
Stenonema ithaca	Light Cahill	10-16			■	■		
Tricorythodes	Trico	20-28				■	■	■
Plauditus	Blue-wing Olive	20-28				■	■	■
Ephemerella dorothea	Sulphur Eastern Pale Even. Dun	16-18			■	■		
Hexagenia limbata	Hex Giant Michigan Mayfly	6-10			■			

Iowa Trout Streams

CADDISFLIES (*Trichoptera*)

Species	Common Name or Imitation	Size	April	May	June	July	August	Sept.
Brachycentrus spp	Grannom Caddis Black Caddis	14-16		■	■	■		
Chimarra sp	Little Black Caddis (Sedge)	16-20			■			
Hydropsyche sp	Spotted Sedge	14-16			■	■	■	
Hydroptilidae spp	Microcaddis	18-22	■	■	■	■	■	■
Glossosomatidae	Tan Sedge	14-16			■	■		
Leptoceridae	Longhorn Sedge	14-18			■	■	■	

Iowa Trout Streams

STONEFLIES (*Plecoptera*) **& MIDGES** (*Diptera*)

Species	Common Name or Imitation	Size	Month					
			April	May	June	July	August	Sept.
Taeniopteryx	Early Brown Stonefly	10-12						
Pterynarcys spp	Giant Black	2-6						
Isoperla spp	Little Yellow Stone Yellow Sally	12-14						
Midges	Tan, Gray, Olive, Yellow, Black	20-28						

49

In the spring, black caddisfly patterns are very productive. As the season progresses, tan or light brown work well.

You should fish with hopper patterns through the summer months and into early autumn, as long as you see the real thing in the grass.

Soft-hackles and Serendipities, like the other wet flies, are fished in the film where they resemble emerging insects that trout intercept just below the surface. It is sometimes hard to tell whether the fish you see rising are taking insects off the surface or from just below the surface. Before you go crazy trying to match a hatch, try tying on an emerger pattern first. Seeing the fish's dorsal fins, but not their heads, in a movement we call "porpoising," is a sure sign they are feeding on emergers.

Big, splashy rises in which the fish come high out of the water often indicate the fish are chasing caddisflies.

Most anglers follow the time-honored practice of using darker flies in off-color water and on dark days. Doing so at least gives you a starting point in fly selection. In high, fast water after a rain, try using scuds, other large wet flies, or a San Juan Worm.

Yogi Berra is quoted as saying, "You can observe a lot by just watching." That pretty well sums up the best approach to learning trout streams and their insects. The more time you spend on the water, the more details you will come to see. It is a skill some of us try to develop consciously to offset the years we've spent outdoors trying to repel, kill, or at least ignore the insects around us.

SUGGESTED FLY PATTERNS

Another common question concerning Iowa trout fishing is: *What flies will I need?* Below is a list of essential patterns. Most of them are familiar old traditionals and available in any fly shop.

This is by no means a complete list of flies. Check with the local fly shops (though there are few) and guides for current information and advice on hatches, patterns and general stream conditions, which often dictate the patterns you'll need.

Pattern Name	Size Range
Dry Flies	
Adams	14 - 24
Blue-wing Olive	16 - 24
Elk-hair Caddis	12 - 18
Hendrickson	12 - 18
Humpy	10 - 16
Light Cahill	10 - 20
Little Black Caddis	16 - 20
Little Yellow Stone	12 - 16
Sulphur	16 - 18
Trico Spinner	22 - 26
Griffith's Gnat	18 - 22
Nymphs & Wet Flies	
Deep Sparkle Pupa	14 - 16
Gold-Ribbed Hare's Ear	12 - 18
Partridge-and-Orange	12 - 16
Pheasant-tail	12 - 18
Prince	12 - 20
Scud	10 - 16
Serendipity	16 - 22
Terrestrials	
Ants	16 - 20
Beetles	10 - 16
Inchworms	10 - 14
Hoppers	8 - 12
Streamers	
Muddler Minnows	4 - 10
Wooly Buggers	4 - 10

Iowa Trout Streams

FISHING SMALL STREAMS

The first season I fly fished, as a ten-year-old with a long split-cane rod, I began each morning by working the entire shoreline of our large farm pond, starting and finishing the circuit always at the same willow tree. One morning by chance I reached the water a little early and saw departing from my customary starting place a large, let's say huge, dorsal fin. The fish had been lying just a couple of feet from shore at the exact spot where I normally planted my feet to start casting. The following morning, nearly trembling, I stopped 20 feet shy of the water, and by false casting off to the side, coaxed out enough line to drop my fly right at the water's edge where I'd seen the fin. Wham! Flashing orange in the morning sun, up came one of the largest bluegills—if not the largest bluegill—I caught in the 35 years we owned the pond.

Today, when I guide, I am careful to be certain my clients understand that when I point out a likely spot it is their fly, not their feet, that I want them to put there. My personal feeling is that most of us are harboring instincts, or at least accumulations of experiences, that will lead us to fish if we follow them with less enthusiasm and more tranquility. Rather than concentrating on stealth, I prefer simply fishing in tempo and in harmony with the waters. Slower, gentler sections, where you see occasional but diligent rises, must be fished with a soft, deliberate touch, while faster, rougher waters can be worked more aggressively.

All of this is said simply to emphasize the fact that by nature trout are extremely wary and humans are often very clumsy.

Upstream and Down

Trout generally face into the current, which means you should fish by casting upstream. If you park at a bridge with a partner and you want to go in opposite directions, the person going downstream should walk well away from the water, just close enough to see what, if anything, is going on. Your choice then is to either walk downstream the entire distance you plan to fish, or to fish individual spots as you find them.

As you move downstream, look for either rising fish or good holding water. When doing that, I stop and cast only to rising fish, meanwhile memorizing the location of promising water to concentrate on as I work back up. On unfamiliar water, exploring in the downstream direction gives you the chance to survey the stream before fishing it.

When fishing upstream you can "prospect" with a nymph and replace it with a dry fly when you encounter rising fish, or you can prospect with a dry fly. Even in the absence of rising fish and obvious insect activity, fish will

Iowa Trout Streams

rise to dries. This is, of course, especially true in the hot months when terrestrials are plentiful.

There are some who believe that you should only fish dry flies, upstream, to rising fish. This strategy, sometimes called the "English dry-fly code," may sound too "purist" for most of us, but it is not without logic and shouldn't be dismissed so quickly. In essence, it's simply a method of sight-fishing. Waiting until you see a rise can prevent you from unnecessarily disturbing the water, and possibly spooking fish before they even get a chance to see your fly.

I frequently fish with anglers who ask what fly to tie on while they are still a mile from the water. Many are so eager to start fishing that in their enthusiasm they drive away fish that might be caught by using a more conservative approach.

The first thing I do when I approach a new spot is wait and watch. It's amazing how often you will see activity after three or four minutes. For me, casting to a sighted fish is the essence of fly fishing's appeal.

When you wade upstream in strange waters, even polarized glasses won't prevent you from wasting time on water that, when viewed from a different angle such as the bank above, is obviously too slow and shallow to hold fish under normal circumstances. That same water might be teeming with fish in the evening when there is a hatch, but during warm days the fish will be in deeper pools and runs nearby. Some Iowa streams have as few as two or three good pools in the course of a mile, and a novice can spend an entire day carefully fishing barren water.

If a stream is unfamiliar to you, take a hike and assess the waters before you start fishing in earnest, but be sure that you and your shadow stay a respectable distance from the water.

Likewise — and I think this is important — when you first locate a new stream, explore from your car in all possible directions before deciding where to begin. My unfortunate first excursion to Iowa trout country was memorable in that it was the first time ever that I fished too much and drove too little. To this day I devote a portion of each trip to exploring both on foot and on wheels.

The object of all this walking and exploring is to find holding water, the water where the fish live (as opposed to the water where, for example, they go out to dinner). Trout need relatively cool, highly oxygenated water. It isn't only the coolness of the water that makes it appealing to trout, but the ability of cold water to retain oxygen better than warm water. Trout can tolerate higher water temperatures if the stream is oxygenated by frequent riffles. Always look for fish where the fresh water comes into the head of a pool, and don't be surprised if you find fish holding in the fast current just below the tail of the pool. If you are fortunate you might spot their fins sticking out of the water before you spook them.

THE NATURE OF SMALL STREAMS

Small streams are similar in a way to a model railroad. Model railroaders take great pains to build everything to scale—the buildings are the correct size in relation to the trains, and so forth. But fitting the display into a room requires the modeler to abandon the scale as it applies to the distance between towns. The scene has to be compressed. That is the way I view small streams. They are large streams with the "air squeezed out."

Following is stream terminology as I use it, plus some tips on how fish relate to the nature of the stream.

Riffles, the little rapids that make up a sizable length of most streams, are high in oxygen but cause the fish to work harder while in them. You generally find fish there in the evenings when they come into the riffles because of a heavy hatch.

Pools are comparatively deep water with a relatively calm surface, with either a run or a riffle at each end. The upstream end is called the head and the downstream end the tail. If there is a riffle coming into the pool you know that the turbulence of the riffle will contribute oxygen in that area. Be careful not to overlook pools because of their size. I can think of several on Spring Branch Creek that are barely large enough to submerge a kitchen chair, yet they hold numerous large browns.

Runs are long, narrow stretches much like pools, but with a swifter current that is sometimes belied by the relatively smooth surface. If deep enough to remain cool they hold fish well. Because of the current they often have undercut banks, which are the classic hiding places for the big ones. There are often weeds hanging out over the water, which makes a run an ideal place to cast a hopper pattern.

If either a pool or a run is situated on a bend or curve in the stream, look for the deepest water to be on the outside of the curve. There is an adage used by rivermen that holds true more often than not: "The steep side's the deep side." The side that has the higher bank is likely to have the deeper water.

Holes and Pocket Water

More common in vernacular than print is the term "hole." When I say "a hole," I mean a diminutive pool, sometimes unpredictably situated. The holes in which I frequently find fish are those where the creek bends sharply around a tree, gouging a deep hole and exposing the tree's roots. Like any pool that is unapproachable from below, you might try fishing this type of hole from upstream, using a weighted nymph and feeding line out quickly as the current takes it into the hole.

Small, sheltered calm spots in otherwise rough water are called "pockets." They are usually situated above or below a rock or deadfall in midstream. Long stretches of "pocket water" are common in mountainous states like Colorado, where the pockets afford the fish protection from the current yet accessibility to food that happens to pass.

Good, fish-holding water may make up only a small percentage of any given stream, and may be limited to only a few pools. Learning to identify this water comes only through spending time on the water.

Stream Improvements

Increasingly, you can expect to find signs of human intervention on the streams. Through the years, people have done a variety of things to prevent bank erosion and to increase the number of places where fish can hold. One bank of French Creek is supported partly by discarded tires. It is common these days to find the banks stabilized with rip-rap, which simply means good-size rocks. Rip-rap can be an eyesore until nature finishes the landscaping job.

Bank hides, or lunker structures, are man-made substitutes for naturally undercut banks, but they have the advantage of being resistant to collapse. Often it is hard to tell rip-rap from a bank hide, and bank hides can be deceptive. I know of one such structure where twice I have had a fish disappear with the full length of my 9-foot leader plus some line and the tip of my rod, too.

Although bank hides made from heavy timbers and covered over to appear natural are generally stable, it is a good idea to watch out for loose rocks or slippery, exposed wood that could cause you to lose your footing.

Iowa Trout Streams

FISHING TO THE WATER

To work any piece of water effectively, begin fishing close to you and work progressively farther out, casting several times in a fan-shaped pattern at each new distance. In still pools, false cast in the air to rid your line of water, even if your fly doesn't need drying, and be sure the false casts are directed so the line and its shadow don't fall over fish (or likely spots for fish). Treat each new section of stream as a puzzle to solve and plan ahead where to place your first, second, third cast, and so forth.

There are as many different angling styles as there are anglers. Some anglers fish nymphs almost exclusively and use very little line, flipping the fly forward just the length of the leader. Others may stay back from the stream to cast a fairly long length of line. Others roll cast frequently.

If you have approached fish quietly from behind and see them close in front of you, let the drift of your fly continue completely over them, nearly to you or, especially with a nymph, even on past you. If at the end of the drift the leader and a little line are still in front of you, a roll cast pickup is in order. If the line passes beyond you downstream, letting the line continue to straighten out for a second will cause the current to load your rod for a good cast back upstream.

Regardless of your personal approach, fish carefully and make as little disturbance as possible. Bear in mind that familiarity with a stream doesn't stop with learning where the fish are, but extends to knowing the best way to work each bit of water. Even in streams only three or four feet wide, the current in the center will be so swift that for your fly to drift along the edge without dragging you must cast from the side you want to fish, not across the current. Take your time. Fish with your rod tip down and your line hand ready. Many novice anglers have more difficulty overcoming line-handling problems than casting problems.

In some situations, the stream might appear barren, and

in your eagerness to find the next pool you may overlook many good holes. On other streams there is such good water and there are so many fish that you must scrutinize the stream literally foot by foot to keep from overlooking the largest fish in the least obvious places.

My approach is to cover carefully any water that looks promising while wasting as little time as possible on marginal water. Don't get so absorbed in studying the water that you forget to look for fish. In a decent stream you should see some fish on a normal day. To learn to see fish more easily, try looking first for their shadows. From bridges you can practice picking out the trout in the huge schools of chubs or suckers. Suckers have white tips on their fins, but so do brook trout. The thing to note is that trout align themselves facing the current precisely, while other fish are often poised at a slight angle.

Casting

To be honest, it is rare that I meet or even observe an angler whose casting skills aren't at least somewhat compromising his or her enjoyment of the sport. But that's nothing to be ashamed of; the same can be said of most golfers. Casting is a lifetime pursuit and, while it's a key factor in the enjoyment of fly fishing, half the fun is the learning process itself. If you don't fish salt water, small streams will likely place the greatest demands on your casting of any type of fishing you do.

Among the common complaints that unsuccessful anglers register with me are wind, high grass and standing weeds along streams, aquatic vegetation in the streams, spooky fish on bright days, and pools that are inaccessible because of overhanging tree branches. Most of these problems diminish not only as your casting skills develop, but also as you get better at approaching the stream. Many casting problems are really problems with your position.

A savvy angler will perform extraordinary maneuvers to approach a worthwhile fish from the best spot. If you study the situation long enough you can usually find a position from which to cast. Sometimes you will select a position and see a better one once you have gotten there.

There are some anglers who will argue, but in my opinion casting is as important as your choice of flies. There is no such think as the "wrong" fly if it's properly presented, whereas a poor presentation with the "right" fly will spook not just one, but many fish.

BE PREPARED, BE POLITE

I'm regularly regaled with tales of woe from anglers who have had a poor trip to the Iowa streams, and more often than not it's because they were not ready for the fishing conditions they encountered. Indeed, anticipating conditions is a skill that can never be totally mastered. From the relatively protected location of my shop, it's easy for me to forget that Saylorville Lake, just fifteen minutes away, is under a small craft advisory. During the three hours it takes me to drive to Manchester, the weather can change drastically, and as important as it might be, weather is just one of the variables that affect success.

In the process of getting ready for a trip, we daydream elaborately of ourselves catching fish, and all too often we arrive to find things not at all as we had imagined them. Having more experience doesn't necessarily mean that we daydream more accurately, but it does mean that with some discipline we can imagine a greater variety of potentially helpful possibilities: Us catching fish in the wind, us catching fish in the rain, us catching fish in crowds of other anglers, and so forth.

In reality, there are so many variables that you can't

anticipate them all. The herd of Holstein cows, for example, is seldom in our daydreams. Or you might arrive at Bloody Run to find that Clayton is the only Iowa county that's had rain in two weeks, and three inches of it fell last night.

Here, then, is some advice on dealing with common "surprises."

WEATHER AND WATER

Trout, already wet and cold and perpetually wary of attack from above, prefer different weather than we do. At least that's a useful way to think about it. The fish themselves probably don't have strong preferences about weather, as such, but rather the protection from view provided by some cloud cover, a little drizzle, or a breeze to ruffle the water's surface. Also entering the equation is the availability of food. The more food there is around, the more daring the fish will be, regardless of visibility. Their survival depends on eating as much as possible while expending the least amount of energy.

When conditions are borderline, a small change can be significant. Once on French Creek, at midday, the rising fish were turning on and off as though someone were flipping a switch. I realized after awhile that scattered, wispy clouds were occasionally darkening the sky just perceptibly, and it was only then that the fish would rise, not when the sun was shining full strength.

FISHING PRESSURE

The easiest way to avoid crowded conditions is the obvious one—fish during the week. If you are restricted by a rigid work situation, consider using a vacation day or two each season. You may not have the stream entirely to yourself, but the pressure should at least be reasonable. Here, in no particular order, are a few recommended times and methods to beat the weekend pressure. The extreme hours I suggest are also some of the best hours for fishing.

Sunday mornings. For reasons ranging from attending church to nursing hangovers, much of humankind isn't available for the trout stream on Sunday mornings. You can be the exception.

Mornings at dawn. Use a flashlight to get to the stream, but don't shine it on the water. You are likely to have the water entirely to yourself, and it's an excellent time to fish. Try stripping a big streamer upstream along the bank hides.

The last hour of daylight. This is my favorite time to fish, and it never fails to surprise me that most folks head for their homes or campfires before it is actually dark. Dusk is also good dry fly time, often with predictable evening hatches. (By that I mean you can predict that there will be an evening hatch and the accompanying dry fly action, not that you can predict what the hatch will be.)

During the long days of summer, fishing with the earliest morning light and latest evening light gives you a good excuse for a nap or a trip to town during the heat of the afternoon when the fishing tends to be off anyway. Carry a light to find your way back to your car in the dark.

Take a hike. That's all there is to it. Most people, even typically industrious ones, don't walk very far to fish. It's amazing how many people you can leave behind with a short hike.

Avoid stocking days. Most local bait anglers keep tabs on the stocking truck, so the more days that have passed since it was last seen, the fewer other anglers there will be. Likewise, don't hesitate to try the streams that the DNR quits stocking in hot weather. The fact that they don't stock them doesn't mean the fish are all gone or dead.

Winter. One January day, after three consecutive days of -20°F, the forecasters rightly predicted 20° above. John Pursell and I were there to catch rising rainbows using a #20 Renegade, Griffith Gnat, or Serendipity, while another angler on the stream was doing well with Gold-Ribbed Hare's Ear nymphs.

Autumn. It astounds me how drastically fishing activity drops off when school starts and televised football emerges from hibernation. My harsh opinion is that if you bypass this best, loveliest season, you forfeit the right to complain about summer crowds.

Fish isolated streams. Once you have tried some of the streams I recommend as the "best," seek out and try others. On any trip, everybody from innkeepers to store clerks and conservation officers tell me different hot spots, especially after I let it be known that I fly fish. Offhand, I'd say that two out of three or more of the tips contain at least some sound advice.

Wait your turn. I don't mean that you should sit and glare at someone already fishing a pool, but neither should you think that someone else's having been there first has ruined it. Fish recover quickly if a pool, even a calm one, is "rested" for a few minutes. Who knows? Your presentation and fly selection could be just what the fish have been waiting for. An almost continuous parade of anglers can pass trout holding in faster, broken water without spooking them.

ETIQUETTE

No matter what you do, whether in Iowa or elsewhere, there will be times when someone will intrude rudely on your fishing. Often it will be a spin fisherman who doesn't realize how much room fly casting takes or how much area a fly angler can cover from one position. With fly anglers, etiquette is largely a matter of common sense, usually based on the newcomer following the first angler upstream. If the first angler is working slowly, you can go around and ahead of him or her by leaving a substantial distance of stream—a couple of good pools, for example—between you. Just put yourself in that person's shoes.

The more anglers on a stream, the less space gets left between them. On the most crowded waters, minimum space between anglers should still leave generous room for casting and playing fish. In this respect, Spring Branch Creek is similar to the Yellowstone River—the next angler might be just 50 feet away, but there are probably scores of fish between the two of you. The only time you fish that close to someone else is when there is no other room, or you're sharing a flask of scotch. You should never crowd another angler just to get to a choice pool.

If it seems appropriate, don't hesitate to clear your intentions by asking. Often the other anglers will give you some tips or invite you to fish even closer than you had intended. The key factor is giving the fish you have disturbed a chance to recover before the next angler gets there.

THE CHANGING LANDSCAPE

There is very little I can recommend that will help you prepare for changes in the streams themselves. You simply have to be mentally prepared. If your last visit to a pool was in the spring, be ready for grass and weeds up to your shoulders in late summer. Last year's nicely cut alfalfa field could be head-high corn this season. Wet or dry seasons will create and destroy pools. Beaver dams appear in places you would never expect. Huge logs in the stream wash away, or trees topple into the stream.

If there is a new suggestion to add here, it is that you take your bearings from permanent, or at least enduring, landmarks. Don't think of a particular riffle as being next to the cornfield. Instead, look for a rock formation to help you return to the spot. This is true also in merely finding the stream. Fields and even buildings can be fickle landmarks. There is a certain left-hand turn that I habitually make, right where the white fence used to be.

PRIVATE LAND

Many streams run through private land. Some begin on state-owned land and continue on through private land. We all know enough not to litter, but even more important to farmers is the preservation of their fences. The stiles, which constitute a standing invitation to fish in the stream without asking, are actually there to protect the fence. Please, don't cause a landowner to close a section of stream because you damaged his fences. I'm very leery of opening gates, but if you determine that it is alright to go through a particular gate, close it immediately, exactly the way it was originally fastened (which means you have to look at it very carefully beforehand).

When in doubt, ask permission.

PART 2

THE TROUT STREAMS OF IOWA

Iowa Trout Streams

Never underestimate the value of a good map and compass.

GETTING AROUND

Every stream that appears on the Iowa DNR's map of trout streams is included in this section. I have organized them into chapters representing more or less logical geographic areas, and beyond that I have devoted more attention to the streams I consider best for fly fishing. These are the streams that have shown an ability to sustain good fish populations, year around, under almost all conditions.

In general, the streams seem to improve the farther north and east you travel, but there are several things to consider when deciding on what makes a stream "good." For example, many of the streams run through parks. These parks range in size from the small county parks that are little more than a mowed picnic area, to the large state parks that are fully equipped recreational areas. Though few of these "park streams" would be the ultimate destination on a "serious" fly-fishing trip, they shouldn't be categorically dismissed. The streams, after all, probably were the reason, or at least one of the reasons, the parks came into being in the first place. Indeed, there are times, or at least I feel there should be, when the quality of the trout stream is secondary to the quality of the picnic area or the playgrounds, when the colorful villages with antique shops and riverboats become an acknowledged part of our enjoyment of trout country.

Similarly, there's a value to campgrounds with trout streams running through them. Just as it's fun to wet a line when you stop at a county park for a picnic lunch, so is it nice to take your rod for an evening stroll while the coals burn down under the grill. I also find it especially pleasant to go out barefoot, carrying nothing but a rod, and make a few casts while the morning coffee perks.

I also have an affinity for what I call "pasture streams." Though some of the very best streams run through pastures, there are several that are characterized by slow-moving water that is often too warm to be stocked in the summer months. While not prime destinations, they share the advantage of providing unrestricted casting space. The deeper holes in them are popular with bait anglers, but you can usually find a few sharp bends that create faster water with pockets that hold fish. From late autumn until early spring, you may finds fish inhabiting some of the slower water that they had to abandon in the heat of summer.

MAPS AND SIGNS

The official trout map distributed by the Iowa Department of Natural Resources is indispensable. Because it is based on

Protected Streams

maps that are primarily road maps, however, it gives only a sketchy view of the streams themselves. At times it's difficult even to tell which side of the road the stream is on. The streams are best depicted on the U.S. Geological Survey's topographical maps. Those, of course, show streams and roads in great detail, but they rarely include the name or number of a road, and their scale requires you to buy several of them just to cover a small area.

The maps I have included here were produced by transcribing the roads and streams from the topographical maps and adding road designations from the transportation maps and, more importantly, from personal experience. Remember this: When you try to navigate the back roads with any map, be aware that the county road numbers or names are not posted where you would expect to find them. Sometimes they are not posted at all.

Part of the problem stems from the fact that to initiate the Emergency 911 telephone system, every street in a township had to be assigned a name or number. Thus you find 340th Avenue about as far from a town as you can get in Iowa. For some reason there are now county roads that are marked with street names on traditional street signs, while the pentagon-shaped county road signs have disappeared. For example, Clayton County Road W67 might be marked only with street signs indicating "St. Sebald Road," while maps may still designate it as W67. Signs will undoubtedly continue to change, but what won't change is their sporadic and, apparently, capricious use.

The new naming and numbering system for roads uses, where possible, "Avenue" and "Drive" to indicate north-south routes, while "Street" and "Road" are used to indicate east-west routes. I've tried to be careful in the text, but if you find an inconsistency, don't worry. In no case that I know of has the state used the same name as both a "road" and a "drive."

For years the DNR marked trout waters with attractive signs—some of them wooden—painted brown with yellow lettering. Although a few of them have survived, they now mean virtually nothing except that at one time the stream was stocked and open to the public. Since the use of signs has been discontinued, anglers must rely on the map and the presence of ladders, called stiles, over the fences to determine whether or not they have located the fishable section of a stream. Very often the stiles are not visible from the road. In the summer you usually can see a path through the weeds leading to these fence crossings, but at other times of the year you have to go slowly and search along fences and down steep banks to find the access.

Remember that the three-way relationship between anglers, the DNR, and landowners is continually changing. My recommendation is that you take "No Trespassing" signs seriously, and that you do your part to prevent new ones from cropping up.

You often can get a clue to a stream's location from either the state's small green and white Game Management Area signs, or, on the main roads, from the brown-and-white Conservation Commission signs that point toward public areas.

Because the maps in this book are large in scale, the curves in the road do not appear to be as sharp as they are in reality. The twists and bends in the stream, however, are more easily followed by being enlarged and are, for the most part, quite accurate.

FINDING YOUR WAY

Since my earliest days of driving Iowa's back roads I have used an auto compass. The times I've driven a car or truck without one, I've missed it or even regretted it. I'm no stranger to remote areas, and I keep my bearings pretty well, but before and after daylight hours, or even on a

Iowa Trout Streams

cloudy day, it's disturbingly easy to lose your bearings on winding roads.

Keep your gas tank filled. The last time I got lost was before dawn when I had to abandon my planned route because of a gasoline crisis I could have easily avoided. On another occasion, I ran completely dry right at dark. Some towns don't have a gas pump, and those that do might keep shorter hours than you think they should. Be sure to fill on Saturday night in case the stations along your route are closed on Sunday morning. This is, after all, a rural area.

On foot, there is always the chance of getting lost if you don't retrace your exact route along a stream. If you try to take a "short cut" by walking straight back to your car, be careful that you don't encounter and follow a different stream than the one you were originally fishing. Hilltops pose a similar problem. If you head down the wrong ravine from a hilltop, you can find yourself at the foot of the hill, but on a road miles from your car. Northeast Iowa isn't the predictable checkerboard of roads and fields that characterizes most of the state. It doesn't hurt to notice periodically features on your back trail and keep track of the number of streams and fences you cross.

There are two basic approaches to fishing many of the streams: you can drive around in your car and fish the obvious holes close to the road, or you can set out and fish the entire length of the water. Both methods have merit. When you elect to fish the entire length of a stream, consider taking a day pack with a rain jacket, a light lunch, and most important, water. Most of us neglect to carry and drink enough water when hiking.

Among the more rugged treks on Iowa's streams are the protected area of Bloody Run and the lower section of French Creek. Those places and others could be approached sensibly with two vehicles, leaving one at a place upstream where you plan to finish fishing the stream.

However you approach these streams, I hope you'll take

the time to look up from the water and enjoy the unique and timeless beauty of these rugged valleys. Explore the small towns and talk to the local residents. There's a deep sense of solitude and history here that can only be discovered if you return often, and linger for a while.

Iowa's Protected Streams

Spring Branch • Ensign Hollow • Bloody Run • South Pine • Upper & Lower French Creek

The streams in this chapter carry special regulations limiting the number or species of trout you can keep, or prohibiting it all together. These regulations are designed to promote and protect populations of naturally reproducing trout. Though these special fisheries are scattered throughout the trout region of Iowa, I have placed them in their own separate chapter for several reasons. The first reason is that they are truly special streams and stand out among the others for their wild trout. Second, it is easy to stumble onto these streams in the course of your traveling and overlook their special status, and risk keeping fish illegally. Third, one of them, Spring Branch, is well suited for the beginner and the experienced angler alike, and for this reason, I have created a more detailed map of Spring Branch to help you explore its waters more successfully.

This isn't to suggest that the "catchable" fisheries are not as good—some, in fact, may be *better*—it is simply to highlight the unique qualities of these protected streams.

Through the years, stretches of various streams have been protected at one time or another. It takes more to change regulations on streams than just the DNR's recommendation; the agency can't simply send conservation officers out to put up or take down signs. The procedure, second in bureaucratic complexity only to changing an actual state law, includes public hearings and takes about two years. Even so, by the time you read this book there may again have been changes affecting which areas are either protected or not protected by special regulations.

Protected Streams

SPRING BRANCH CREEK

In addition to being Iowa's premier trout stream, Spring Branch is the site of the state's only trout hatchery, Manchester Fish Hatchery, one of the oldest in the nation. (The other two facilities—Decorah and Big Spring—are rearing stations.) The history of the facility began in the late 1800s when the federal government, in search of locations for new hatcheries, deemed it the best of the more than 50 sites they identified and studied in Nebraska, South Dakota, and Iowa. The hatchery produced and shipped fish to the eastern states until ownership was transferred to Iowa in 1976.

The stream itself is a classic spring creek. It stretches roughly three miles, from the spring head just north of Iowa Route 20, through the grounds of the hatchery, then under County Road D5X, and empties into the Maquoketa River (pronounced mah-KO-keh-tah) at Bailey's Ford county park. The best fishing is found in the first two miles below the spring, the portion of the stream north of D5X. This area is restricted to artificial lures, with a limit on the length of trout you can keep. It is the most "developed" stream in the state in terms of improvements, such as bank hides and bank stabilization. For many years, the Hawkeye Fly Fishing Association (HFFA) maintained and improved the stream. In the late 1990s, the state renewed and added to the improvements, maintaining the stream's status as one of the best in the Midwest.

On the state's trout map, the section just above the confluence of Spring Branch and the Maquoketa is labeled Bailey's Ford. Although the length limit and lure restrictions do not apply here, the stream still holds some nice fish, and the campground is a great place to stay on overnight trips.

Iowa Trout Streams

The infamous wall at the Manchester Fish Hatchery on Spring Branch Creek.

Protected Streams

FISHING SPRING BRANCH

Spring Branch (often referred to simply as "Manchester") is frequently described with a single adjective—*tough*. Like many catch-and-release streams across the country, the challenges it poses are both natural and man-made. Spring creeks are, by nature, tricky—the water is so clear and smooth that on a sunny day the fish can scrutinize everything from your fly to your haircut. The simple act of keeping the shadow of your line away from the fish can be a problem. Also difficult is achieving a drag-free drift of any length. Though the stream is tiny by anyone's definition, its natural twists and turns, plus the additional dynamics created by the bank hides, result in complex currents that demand accurate casting and diligent line mending.

In addition to these natural challenges is the problem of the fish themselves. Like the fish in all so-called "trophy" streams, the fish here are savvy. They see more flies in a year than most of the anglers who fish here. To combat this problem, anglers through the years have tried using smaller and smaller flies, but my assessment of the problem is that the fish are not spooked by the fly any more than they are by the leader. That is to say, they are "leader shy." As an alternative to tiny flies, I recommend using fluorocarbon tippet material.

In spite of the fact that it requires skill rising to a level that some anglers have dubbed "technical" fishing, Spring Branch is still the stream I most often recommend to beginners. For anglers just getting started, the frustration of not catching fish pales in comparison to the frustration of not finding fish. Although it might be tough to hook and land large fish here, there is seldom a problem locating fish. It's rare not to find find rising fish somewhere in the creek, even in the dead of winter. While the resident fish are what I call "Ph.D. fish," there are generally enough recent escapees from the hatchery that even a beginner can be successful.

More experienced anglers can use Spring Branch to hone their fishing skill to a fine edge. Many Midwestern anglers have experienced immediate success on famous Western rivers like Idaho's Henry's Fork and Colorado's Frying Pan because of disciplines learned on Spring Branch Creek and other streams like it.

So important do I consider this stream that I have drawn a "treasure map" to facilitate your first visits. After you've made a few visits, I encourage you to explore harder, looking for trophy fish where you least expect them. Spring Branch epitomizes the cliche of not being able to see the forest for the trees. Here, there are so many fish in sight that you have trouble focusing on individual fish.

On the other hand, you can't overestimate a trout's ability to conceal itself in a spring creek. Once, fly-tackle manufacturers' representative and former Yellowstone guide, Kurt Weieneth, and I were discussing, in great detail, a section of the creek no more than 15 yards long. We finally resorted to drawing on a scrap of paper, and Kurt mapped in great detail the exact location of a grass-covered clump of dirt that sheltered the 19" brown he had failed to catch a week earlier. I hadn't seen the stream in a couple of months, yet I knew in detail the area he was describing.

All of the flies recommended in Chapter 3 work well here. There are brook trout along with the browns and rainbows, particularly near the spring head where you find watercress and, consequently, scuds. A rain storm can bring the creek's level up dramatically, but, unlike a large river, it can return to normal in just a few hours.

During the summer months, Spring Branch is an excellent stream for hopper patterns. In the winter, Griffith's Gnats make convincing snow midge imitations. Fish during the warmest part of the afternoon, regardless of how cold it is overall.

Protected Streams

Spring Branch Creek
Delaware Co.
Delorme p. 33

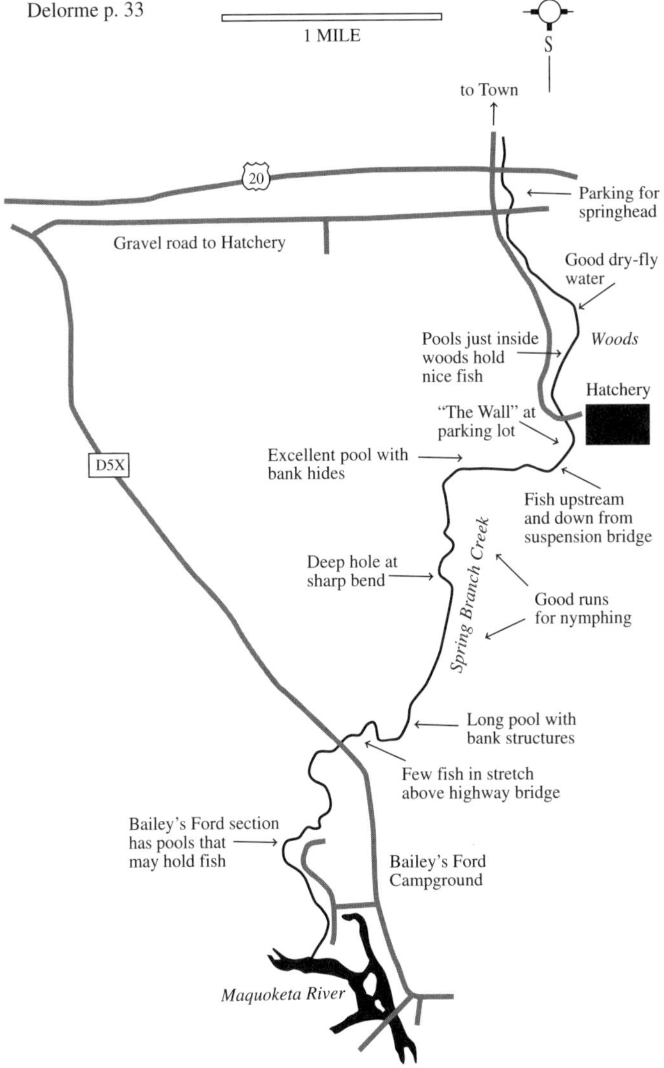

1 MILE

to Town

- Parking for springhead
- Gravel road to Hatchery
- Good dry-fly water
- Pools just inside woods hold nice fish
- Woods
- Hatchery
- "The Wall" at parking lot
- Excellent pool with bank hides
- Fish upstream and down from suspension bridge
- Deep hole at sharp bend
- Good runs for nymphing
- Spring Branch Creek
- Long pool with bank structures
- Few fish in stretch above highway bridge
- Bailey's Ford section has pools that may hold fish
- Bailey's Ford Campground
- Maquoketa River

D5X

81

FINDING SPRING BRANCH

Spring Branch is due west of Dubuque on Route 20. From the east, take the first Manchester exit; from the west, the second. Turn left from the ramp, away from town, and drive south toward Bailey's Ford, for just under a mile. Take the first gravel road going left. Your first and only stop will be at the paved road leading to the hatchery. At that point you'll see a parking area to your left, near the spring house. Turn right to reach the hatchery where the stream skirts the parking lot. Allow yourself time to visit the hatchery before you begin fishing because once you start fishing you'll find it hard to quit before you absolutely have to.

Spring Branch Creek makes an ideal one-night outing. Camping at Bailey's Ford is convenient, and Manchester is a pleasant town with several motels and a variety of places to eat. To reach town from the hatchery you don't need to retrace your route on the gravel; just take the blacktop out of the hatchery and follow it under the four-lane until you reach the highway, then turn left to go about two miles into town.

Fishing pressure can be heavy at times. I generally fish Spring Branch during the week, leaving Des Moines mid-morning, fishing the evening hatches, and fishing again early the following morning before starting home. The adventure takes little more that 24 hours, yet it feels like two days of fishing.

If you fish this stream when it feels crowded to you, be patient and courteous and you will get a turn at every pool. Most anglers depart before that prime final hour of light. Carry a flashlight and fish until it is absolutely too dark to continue.

Protected Streams

ENSIGN HOLLOW

In the early 1990s, Ensign Hollow received extensive HFFA work similar to that of Spring Branch Creek. Today, the creek receives mixed reviews from visiting anglers. Ensign Hollow resembles two totally different streams that have been joined end-to-end. Your opinion of the stream will depend on which section you fish.

Once you get to Ensign Hollow, follow the lane upstream to the small parking area, which is roughly in the middle of the stream's length. You'll pass the lower section, which winds through private pasture land. Except for a few thistles, it is like a golf course, only better because it has trout.

Upstream from the parking area, the land is owned by the state. This is the section to which the improvements have been made, and your ability to fish here depends largely on whether or not the banks have been mowed. I find this schizophrenic little stream to be fun, even when the grass and weeds are tall.

The lower section holds more fish than you might expect. As usual, keep a lookout for rising fish, and drift a fly through some of the deep bends. The upper section, with all the streamside vegetation, is better suited for terrestrials—ants, beetles and hoppers.

Overall, there is a good fish population. Though Ensign Hollow may never be another Spring Branch, it enjoys the same protective regulations and should only get better with each passing season.

FINDING ENSIGN HOLLOW

Even more challenging than fishing Ensign Hollow is finding it. The creek lies in southwestern Clayton county, about 18 miles north of Manchester, as the crow flies. If you're traveling north from Manchester, take Route 13 to Strawberry Point, then go west to the second road going north (or right). Don't look for signs to tell you it is W67, which it really is, because all signs say St. Sebald Road. The road reverses its course once, but stay with it without taking any turns suggested by other signs pointing to St. Sebald. Just follow the straightest route you can take. You should pass, not turn onto, these roads: 345th to the left, 342nd to the right, and 338th to the right. The next left is 322nd, which follows the creek upstream.

Protected Streams

Ensign Hollow
Clayton Co.
DeLorme p. 32

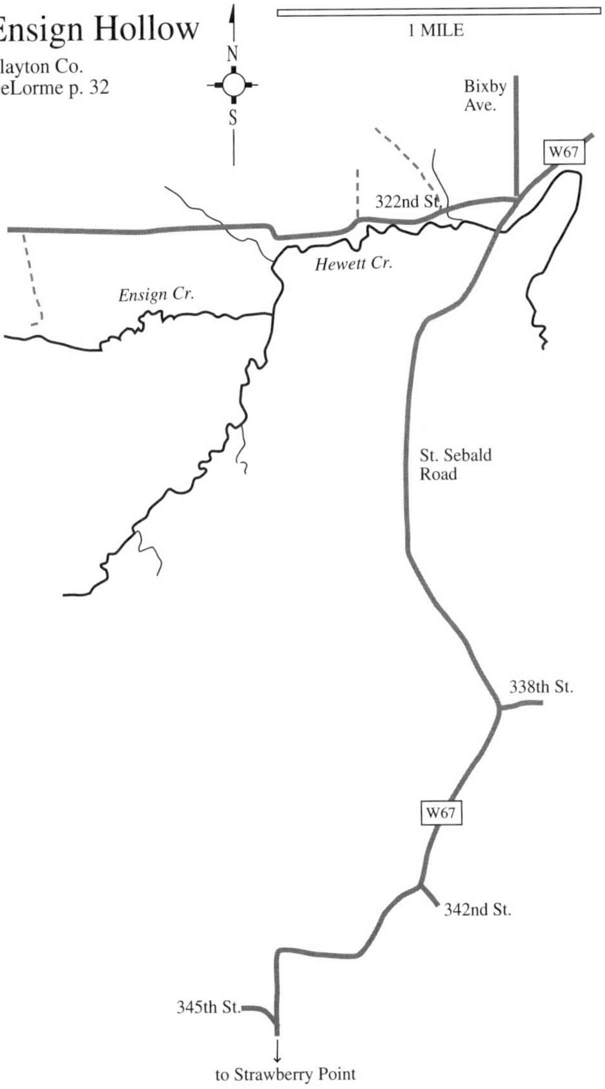

BLOODY RUN

This creek is a long, put-and-take stream with a protected section roughly four miles long in the middle. There was a time when no part of the stream was protected, and there were some years when the upper section carried special regulation; even the lower portion was protected for a while. Of the streams discussed in this book, this, at least in places, is the most like a river. There are places along Bloody Run that remind me of stretches of Yellowstone Park's Gallatin and Gibbon Rivers. If you walk into the middle section of Bloody Run from Jade Avenue, the steep hike would make a good "rehearsal" for a Western trip. If you do hike in this way, the area is remote enough that a sprained ankle would make getting back to your car a serious ordeal.

Though it seems to be off-color more often than the other streams, Bloody Run has good diversity of water. You can be fishing along in waters similar to most of our other creeks and then come upon a pool the size of a small farm pond. Make sure you have streamers and woolly buggers with you.

FINDING BLOODY RUN

Bloody Run is just west of the town of McGregor, which stands on the banks of the Mississippi at the intersection of Highways 18 and 76. To find the creek, follow U.S. 18 west from McGregor. Two paved "loops" veer away from the highway to the north and then quickly rejoin it (see map, opposite page). These are sections of the old highway. The loop closest to town, marked 145th Street, is a possible, but difficult, route to the eastern end of the protected section of Bloody Run. The trail that appears on my map as Jade Avenue is marked as a "Level B Service" road, which tells me that it is still public. The "no trespassing" signs that the

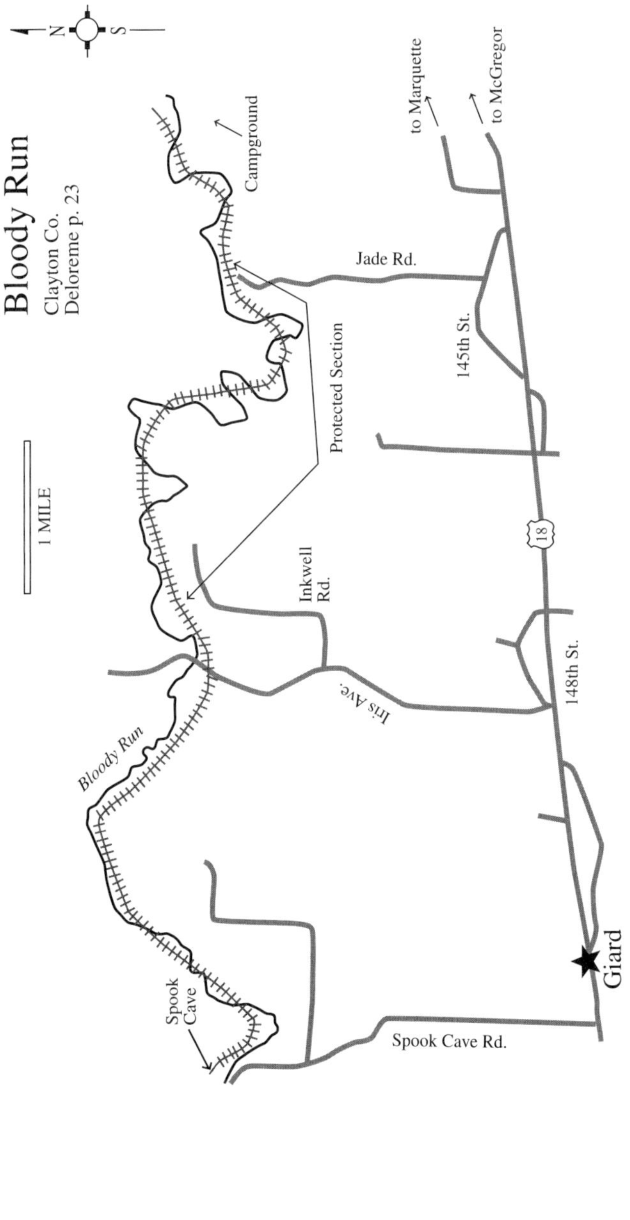
Bloody Run
Clayton Co.
Deloreme p. 23
N
S
1 MILE
Campground
to Marquette
to McGregor
Jade Rd.
Protected Section
145th St.
18
Inkwell Rd.
Iris Ave.
148th St.
Bloody Run
Spook Cave
Giard
Spook Cave Rd.

homeowners have posted on either side of it tell me that they wish it weren't—and, more importantly, they tell me that the landowners really don't want you parking on their property.

The next loop to the west, 148th Street, is the route to the western end of the protected section. Iris Avenue takes you to a bridge that crosses the stream at a public access. There was a time when Inkwell Road could be used (it's another steep hike, like Jade Avenue), but the last time I looked it was in terrible condition.

Lower Bloody Run. Although not protected, there is good fishing and excellent camping at the lower end of Bloody Run. Follow U.S. 18 into Marquette and follow signs to the park.

Upper Bloody Run. Follow the signs to Spook Cave. Unlike other streams, however, the upper reaches of Bloody Run are not the best.

Protected Streams

SOUTH PINE

The rigorously protected, self-sustaining population of brook trout in South Pine has been the subject of intense speculation and substantial scientific investigation. According to DNR records, the stream has never been stocked, and genetic testing of the trout that are present in the stream indicates that these fish are indeed unique, or at least not related to any brookies the state has ever used in its stocking program. I have received calls from people fervent in their belief that these are descendants of fish that inhabited these same waters in pioneer days, and there is certainly no way to prove otherwise. Nor is there reason to disbelieve that these are survivors from the last Ice Age. I think they probably are, but I also know that humans have a nearly compulsive tendency to move fish around, so the question will remain unanswered.

The state of Iowa, with initial assistance from the Iowa Natural Heritage Foundation, was able to acquire land in order to protect it. In addition, the fisheries people have taken steps to relocate individual members of this trout population and also to hatch eggs collected from them. The resulting fingerlings have been stocked in selected, suitable areas.

Fortunately for the trout, this stream is the most difficult to get to of all the streams in this book. It's a very small stream, and it fills with vegetation by early summer. I recommend you approach South Pine as a naturalist rather than an angler. For this reason, I have not included a map of South Pine. If you're interested in visiting this little creek, consult the Iowa DNR map.

UPPER AND LOWER FRENCH CREEK

The most dramatic change to the roster of protected waters was the 1997 addition of French Creek. Prompting the new restrictions was official documentation of what many of us already knew: Brown trout were reproducing in the stream naturally. What the DNR determined that the rest of us didn't know was the regularity of the spawning. Systematic study showed that the stream-born fish didn't result from a chance spawning or two, but from several years of consistent reproduction.

Another distinguishing feature of French Creek is that the upper portion is one of the places where the Pine Creek brook trout have been introduced.

Because of what, to me, is its logical geographic relation to Waterloo Creek and North and South Bear, French Creek is discussed later (page 102).

Protected Streams

The beautiful—and challenging—French Creek in Allamakee County.

Iowa Trout Streams

An inviting stretch of South Bear Creek near Highlandville.

THE NORTHERN TRIANGLE

WATERLOO CREEK • NORTH BEAR CREEK • SOUTH BEAR CREEK • FRENCH CREEK

Tucked away in the hilly northeastern corner of Iowa's trout country, in one of the most beautiful parts of the state, are three of Iowa's best and most popular trout-fishing destinations—French Creek, Waterloo Creek, and North and South Bear creeks. Combined, they are a favorite destination of anglers from the Twin Cities, Madison, Chicago and, of course, Iowa. I've dubbed them the Northern Triangle, and it's not unusual for anglers to fish all three in one trip, or even in a single day.

Along the base of the Northern Triangle are three large towns—Decorah, Waukon and Lansing—that have good motels and restaurants. There also are campgrounds, general stores and motels off the beaten path, and more towns (and trout streams) just across the border in Minnesota.

If you find yourself visiting this area frequently, take the time to learn the back roads. This chapter gives directions for taking back roads from French Creek to Waterloo Creek, from Waterloo to North and South Bear, and from North and South Bear to French Creek. That means that you may need to reverse the order of some instructions.

The Northern Triangle

WATERLOO CREEK

Framed by lofty wooded hills on one side and the straight, rocky spine of Waterloo Ridge on the other, Waterloo Creek winds its way from Minnesota through a long valley of mostly closely grazed pastures skirted by a gravel road.

There was a time when my diminutive 1966 Yellowstone travel trailer was parked about ten steps from the creek in the campground at the western edge of Dorchester. It was my home away from home when I was writing the first edition of this book. I chose this spot because Waterloo Creek, in addition to being one of the best trout streams in Iowa, is midway between French Creek and North Bear. By traveling the back roads, Waterloo Creek is within 15 or 20 minutes of the two others.

To begin learning the stream, locate the three bridges: one at the south end of Dorchester, another modern concrete one about a mile from the Minnesota border, and an old, steel truss bridge almost at the border. (Across the border, Waterloo Creek becomes Bee Creek.) Look for fish in both directions from all three bridges. Between the lower two bridges, just before Homewood Hill Road enters from the right as you head upstream, is a prominent stocking hole where you will sometimes find rising fish that have eluded capture. Don't overlook the stretch immediately below this hole; there are usually fish there, and it can only be fished with a fly rod or ultralight tackle.

It seems downright criminal, but the best fishing is often where you'd rather not fish. On Colorado's famous Blue River, amid the beauty of the Rockies, the best fishing is next to the parking lot of a factory outlet mall in Silverthorn. On Waterloo Creek, in Iowa's picturesque "Little Switzerland," the best fishing is right in the middle of Dorchester. The state's acquisition in the late 90s of land downstream from town has made Waterloo Creek an even more attractive destination than ever.

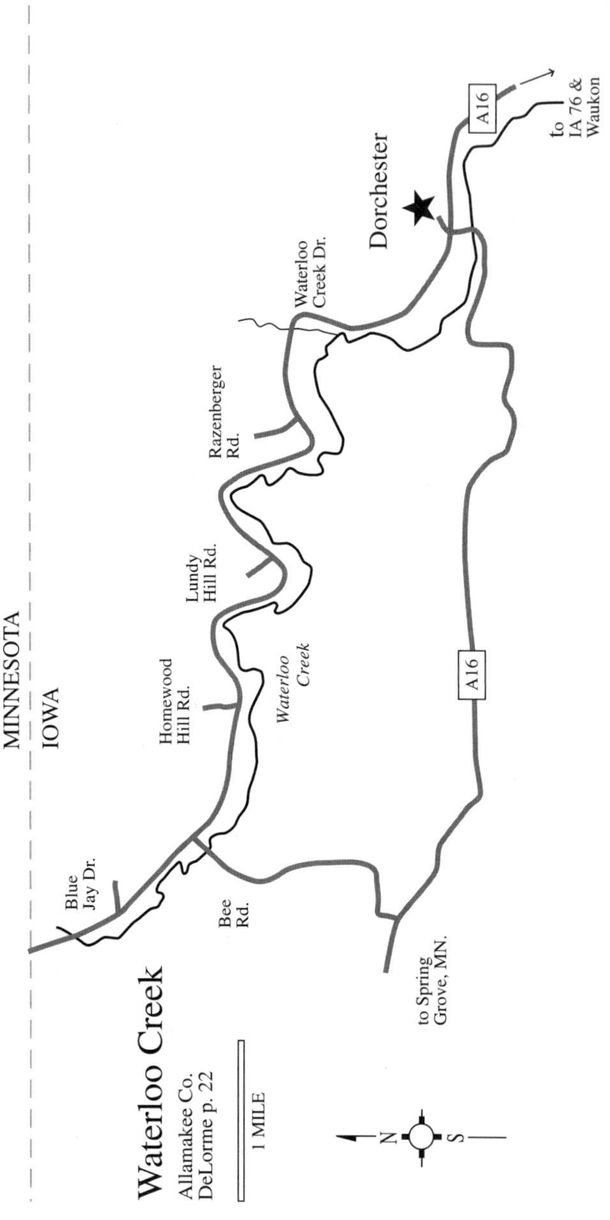
Waterloo Creek
Allamakee Co.
DeLorme p. 22
1 MILE
N
S
MINNESOTA
IOWA
Blue Jay Dr.
Bee Rd.
to Spring Grove, MN.
Homewood Hill Rd.
Waterloo Creek
Lundy Hill Rd.
Razenberger Rd.
A16
Waterloo Creek Dr.
Dorchester
A16
to IA 76 & Waukon

The Northern Triangle

In the upper reaches of Waterloo anglers will have to drift heavily dressed dry flies, soft-hackles, or even scuds over holes in the watercress. Some of the sections are so delicate you have to false cast to rid your line of water droplets that would spook the fish on your next cast.

FINDING WATERLOO CREEK

Follow State Highway 76 north out of Waukon and turn left on A16. Where A16 turns left onto the bridge that crosses the creek, keep going straight into town. This is the first bridge referred to above. There are crossovers to the stream on both sides of the bridge. Dorchester has a small store and a couple of places to eat, one of which is the Sportsmen Motel just north of town on Route 76. (This is also the road to Caledonia, Minnesota, so if you're coming from the north, simply follow Highway 76 south to the Northern Triangle streams.)

NORTH BEAR

This stream flows southeast in Winneshiek County from the Minnesota border to the Allamakee County line. From what I regard as the "first bridge," (see map, opposite) which marks the confluence with South Bear, you can fish North Bear upstream nearly to the state line. Compressed into its official 4.2-mile length is as much good trout habitat as any other Iowa stream I can think of. There are three more bridges with parking areas above the first one, and each provides easy access to the stream.

Whether you approach from the east or west, you are most likely to intersect North Bear at the first bridge. As you work your way north, watch for rising fish; there is a variety of water suited to both nymph and dry-fly fishing. The third bridge upstream from North Bear's confluence with South Bear is very small, quiet water which flows from the headwaters. It's beautiful, but holds fewer fish.

I don't think I'll be giving away secrets if I say that Ed Powell (grandson and namesake of the cane-rod builder E. C. Powell) ranks North Bear among his favorite Iowa streams. Ed is known to place great faith in Humpies, but here he uses an Elk Hair Caddis. He is also such a remarkable caster that he can work almost any water with almost any fly and catch fish if they are present. I pass this information along as an endorsement, not just of the stream and the fly, but of casting practice as well.

SOUTH BEAR

South Bear, which flows along Quandahl Road, can be reached from several small parking areas between Highlandville and the confluence with North Bear. This is excellent fly-fishing water and would receive as much attention as North Bear if it, too, had bridge accesses. I have

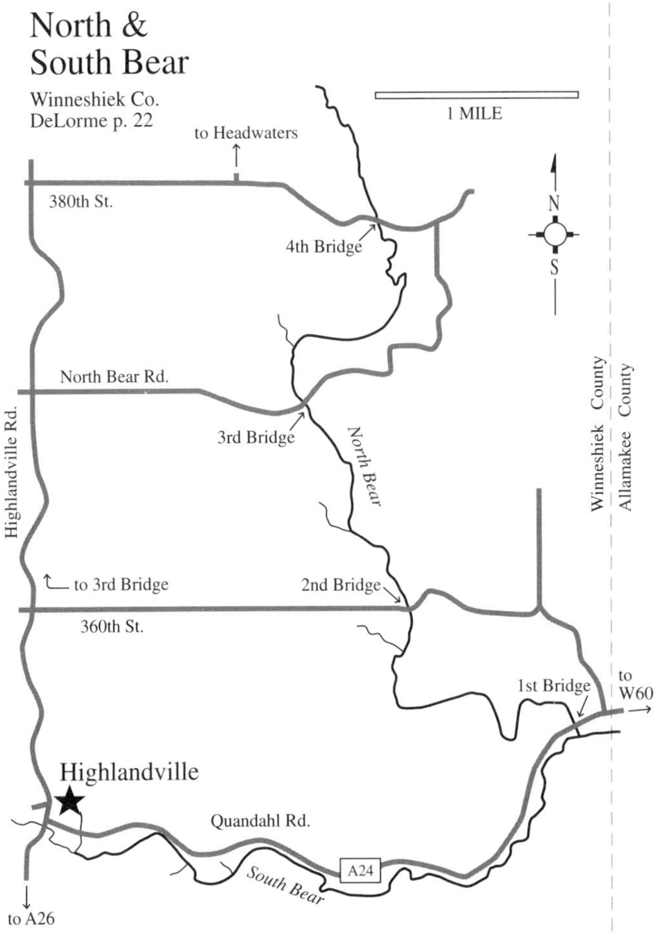
North &
South Bear
Winneshiek Co.
DeLorme p. 22
to Headwaters
1 MILE
380th St.
4th Bridge
N
S
North Bear Rd.
3rd Bridge
North Bear
Highlandville Rd.
Winneshiek County
Allamakee County
to 3rd Bridge
2nd Bridge
360th St.
1st Bridge
to W60
Highlandville
Quandahl Rd.
A24
South Bear
to A26

known South Bear to conceal big fish despite the relentless angling pressure. Though most of the stream boasts excellent habitat unseen by the casual drive-by fishermen, one large brown passed an entire season living in the large pool under the bridge at the Highlandville campground. Hundreds of anglers, veterans and novices alike, either didn't see the fish or failed to tempt it sufficiently.

Despite South Bear's proximity to the road, North Bear is a bit easier to fish and seems to draw somewhat more attention. South Bear's upper stretches (above the campground) are often stocked, unannounced, with brown trout.

FINDING NORTH AND SOUTH BEAR

The hardest part of finding these streams is finding W38 in Decorah. It intersects College Drive just north of the bridge crossing the Upper Iowa River off of Water Street, the main business street. There is a large convenience store there (check your gas gauge), and North Street comes in from the west.

To find this location from State Highway 9, use the map of Decorah (page 109). From the west, go north on U.S. 52 and then right on Fifth Avenue, which will take you past the city campground. From the east, you can take Montgomery Street to Water Street by following signs to the business district and Luther College.

From Decorah, take W38, called Locust Road, toward Highlandville. Do not turn right on A38 (a common mistake). When you get to Locust, bear right onto Big Canoe Road (A26). After about 2.5 miles, just before the Big Canoe Lutheran Church and the large cemetery, bear left onto Highlandville Road, which is shown as A24 on the map, and follow it the remaining one mile into town.

As you enter town, there is a general store on your left and some houses and other buildings on the right that you

The Northern Triangle

probably won't see until after you pass them. I mention this because Highlandville might not immediately match the mental picture you have of a "town."

The general store runs a nice campground where I now keep my old Yellowstone travel trailer. The store sells gasoline (but not necessarily on Sunday). Next to the campground is the only bridge crossing South Bear, and it is here that you turn east on Quandahl Road to follow South Bear (now on your right) to the parking area just before the first bridge across North Bear (see description of the streams above).

From Waterloo Creek: You can reach North Bear by taking A16 west out of Dorchester (which is just off north-south Highway 76) and following it as it angles northwest. Turn left onto W60, Balsam Road, heading back south. Look for two bridges, a one-lane bridge followed by a larger one. It is the road between the bridges, Quandahl Road, that takes you toward Highlandville and the first bridge on North Bear.

If you are on Waterloo Creek upstream from Dorchester, cross the concrete bridge (see Waterloo Creek below) and take Bee Road to reach A16.

To reach French Creek from Highlandville: Follow Quandahl Road past the confluence of the North and South Bear, and continue until it tees into W60 (Balsam). Turning left here will put you on the route to Waterloo Creek just discussed; right will take you toward French Creek. If you turn right, you will immediately cross Bear Creek and arrive shortly at a stop sign. Make the sharp turn to the left (east) and you will be on A26, which takes you to Route 76, just a little south of Dorchester. Turn right onto 76 and watch for A26 to resume on the left (see additional instructions in the section on French Creek).

FRENCH CREEK

French Creek meanders though a beautiful valley, narrow in its upper stretches then broadening out with high limestone outcroppings and cedar-covered hillsides. For wild trout, French Creek is second only to Spring Branch. I've already mentioned the stream and its trout population on page 90, in the chapter on protected streams.

French Creek is designated in two parts, the upper and lower sections, which are divided by a large parking lot that doubles as a primitive camping area. Downstream from the large parking area, near the dairy farm, is a second, smaller parking area. Downstream from there, the creek is accessible from the county road.

Upper French Creek is small water that is intermittently impeded by beaver dams. The valley section of lower French has been allowed to grow wild, making it tough going in the summer months. Still, the beauty of the surrounding, the gin-clear water and the wild brown trout, distinguish French Creek as a tremendously desirable destination.

The Northern Triangle

FINDING FRENCH CREEK

French Creek is southeast of Waterloo Creek. If you're coming south from Dorchester, take Highway 76 to A26 east. Then follow it until it meets County Road X6A, going south. If you're coming up from the south, take State Highway 9, which runs east-west from Lansing through Decorah. Route X6A goes north from State Highway 9 about two miles west of Lansing. At this point X6A is called Four Mile Drive, but it soon merges with Mays Prairie Road. If you are coming from the west (Waukon), you can turn directly north on Mays Prairie Road.

To reach the upper parking and camping area from the south, follow X6A to French Creek Road and turn left (west). Go straight, and after you descend to bottom land the road will turn right while a lane continues straight. Turning to the right takes you to the upper parking lot. Going straight takes you to a separate parking area for fishing the upper portion of the stream.

To reach the parking area at the dairy farm, continue on X6A; it winds downhill as you approach the stream. Watch for signs. The drive to the parking area cuts back hard to the left and drops out of sight. If you reach the bridge where the road crosses the creek at the dairy farm, you will have missed the parking area. From the bridge you can fish up or down the creek. The water immediately upstream from the bridge is good for nymph fishing.

From French Creek, you can get to Waterloo Creek by taking X6A (Mays Prairie Road) north from the dairy farm (downstream) and following it to the right. Signs make it look as if the road becomes Hartley Road, but it changes to Mays Prairie Road again. Whether you are leaving French to get to Waterloo, or vice versa, your goal is to stay on Mays Prairie Road. If you go west at the turn, Hartley takes you immediately to X20, Lycurgus Road, which at this point you don't want. Hey, I told you these were the back roads.

After X6A crosses the Upper Iowa River it meets A26,

which along here is called Iowa River Drive. Turning to the west (left) takes you to Route 76 (about 4 miles), and you turn right to go into Dorchester. You can find A26 coming in from the left and take it to W60 and North and South Bear creeks also (see above).

The Northern Triangle

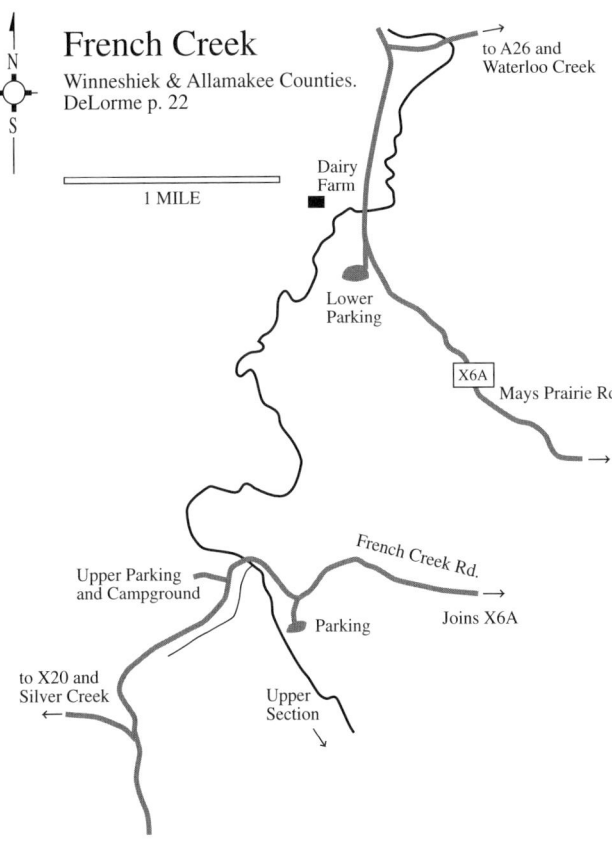

Limestone bluffs rise above Trout Run near Decorah.

DECORAH & THE UPPER IOWA RIVER BASIN

**TROUT RUN CREEK • TWIN SPRINGS •
TROUT RIVER • COON CREEK •
PATTERSON CREEK • SILVER CREEK •
PINE CREEK • WEST CANOE •
COLDWATER CREEK • BIGALK •
BOHEMIAN CREEK**

If there is a geographical "heart" of Iowa trout country, it is Decorah. Decorah is surrounded by streams because of its location on the Upper Iowa River, which flows through the center of town, and into which every stream north of Route 9 feeds, either directly or indirectly. On any state map you can see that the river, though twisty as the proverbial dog's hind leg, flows essentially southeast, then turns abruptly northeast, forming a "V" shape with Decorah at its southern point.

A map of Decorah is included here not only to show the streams that are in town, but more importantly because anyone who spends a lot of time fishing Iowa will inevitably need to find his or her way through this surprisingly complicated, but pretty, little city.

107

TROUT RUN

Trout Run is the source for the water that flows through the Decorah Rearing Station. As with the hatchery at Spring Branch, allow time to walk through the rearing station when you visit here.

To fish Trout Run, follow Trout Run Road down from the rearing station toward State Highway 9. Park at the spot near the remnants of the old railroad trestle, and fish either up or down from there.

FINDING TROUT RUN

On your first visit to Trout Run, look for the intersection of Trout Run Road and Highway 9 on the western edge of town. You can return to town via Siewer's Spring Road or Middle Calmar Road; this will help you learn these shorter, but harder-to-find, routes from town.

Twin Springs, not far from its source near the old hatchery.

Decorah & the Upper Iowa River Basin

Decorah
Trout Run/Twin Springs

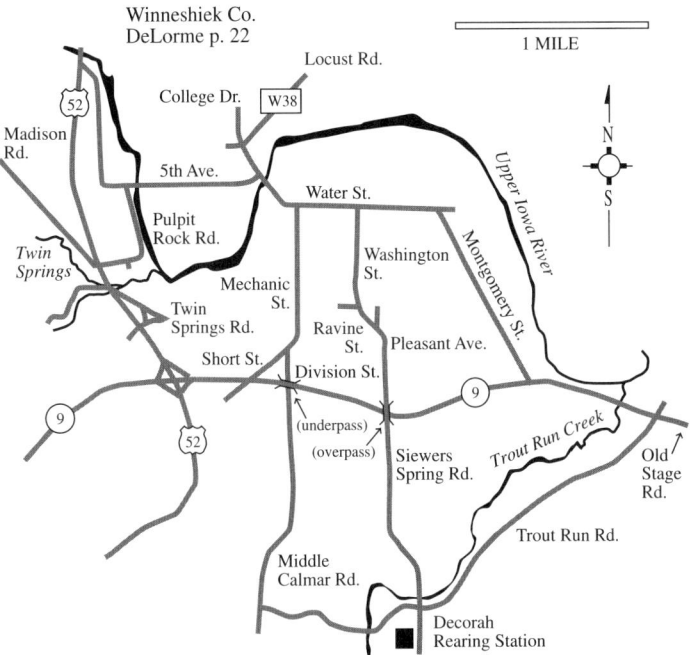

TWIN SPRINGS

Twin Springs flows through a city park and campground on the western edge of Decorah. It is heavily fished because of the campground along its banks, but as a rule it is heavily stocked. As I said before, you might not go out of your way to fish here, but the combination of a decent stream with a good campsite is fine indeed. Upstream you will encounter the old races of an historic hatchery that once stood here. Twin Springs is most easily reached from Twin Springs Road, not from the campground (see map).

Iowa Trout Streams

TROUT RIVER AND COON CREEK

These two streams are located just east of Decorah along a stretch of old Highway 9 that bears a variety of names including Old Stage Road, A52, and, not surprisingly, Old Highway 9. Coon Creek is one of several Iowa streams in which the water quality has been steadily improving as a result of agricultural initiatives aimed at reducing sediment. The amount of sediment in the stream dropped by more than forty percent in just a short period in the late 1990s. Trout River is an easy-to-find, coldwater pasture stream. Like Coon Creek, it is stocked throughout the summer months.

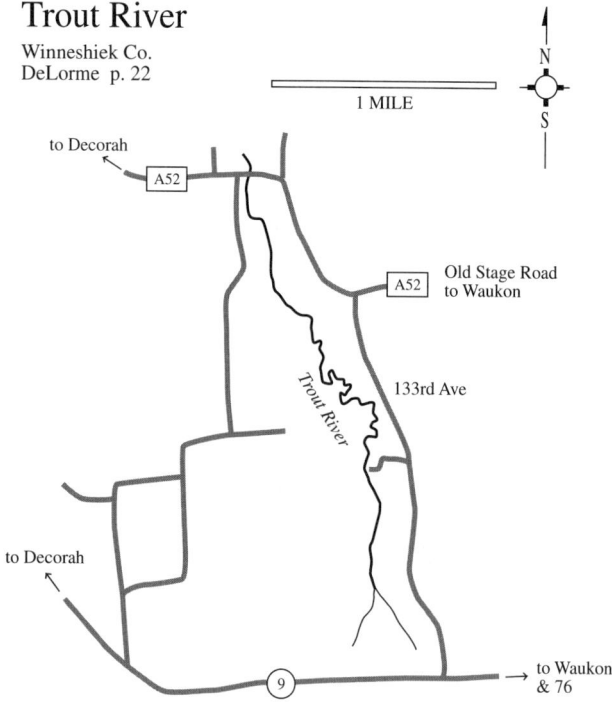

Decorah & the Upper Iowa River Basin

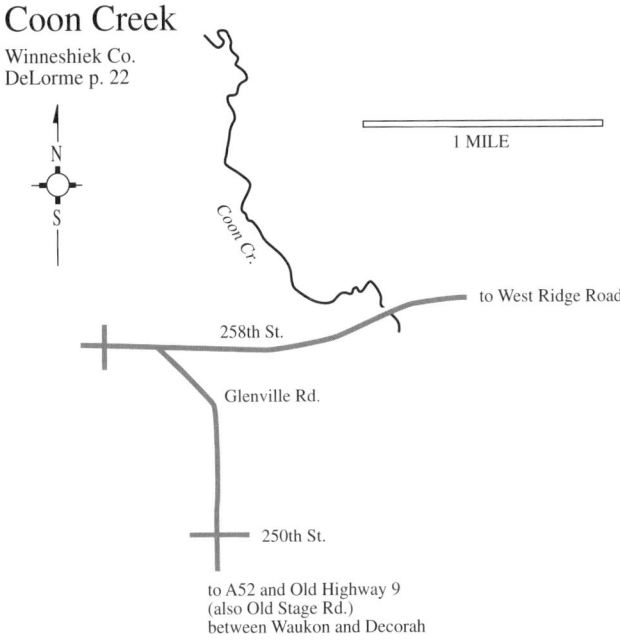

FINDING TROUT RIVER AND COON CREEK

In Decorah, pick up Old Stage Road from River Road, which runs north from (new) Route 9, directly across the street from where Trout Run Road meets Route 9 coming from the rearing station. North of Route 9, Old Stage Road turns off to the east toward Waukon. Three and a half miles east of Decorah, Trout River flows right under Old Stage Road, and access to the stream is a scant mile east of the bridge (turn south on 133rd Avenue). A little farther to the east is a large stone church, Glenwood Lutheran, and shortly thereafter is Glenville Road. To get to Coon Creek, turn north and proceed past 250th Street to 258th Street and turn right. Less than a mile farther on is the creek and the long drive leading to the parking area.

Iowa Trout Streams

To locate these streams from Waukon, follow Main Street out of town to the west. It's called Old Highway 9 or A52. The turnoff to Coon Creek is about seven or eight miles away, depending on where you start counting. The turn should be marked with a sign.

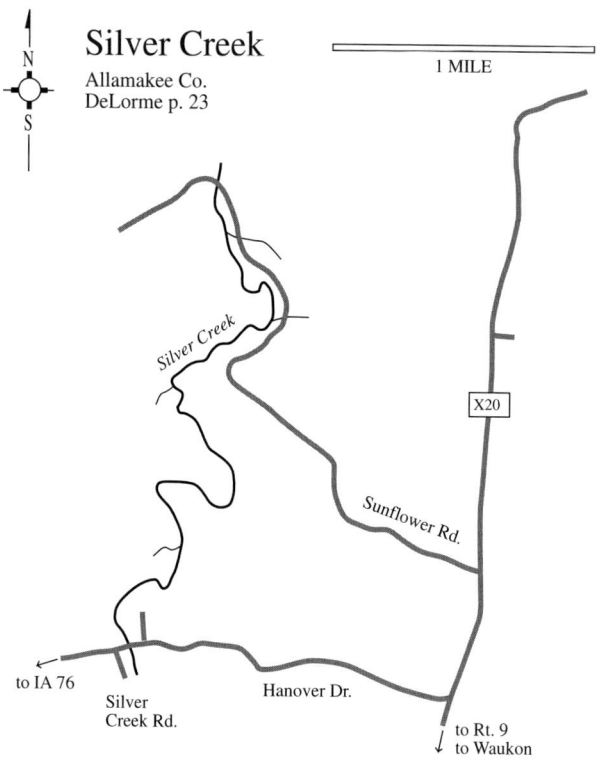

Decorah & the Upper Iowa River Basin

PATTERSON, SILVER AND PINE

These three streams often are side trips for anglers fishing the better-known streams that make up the Northern Triangle. They are all accessed most easily from Route 76, which runs north from Waukon toward the Minnesota border and is a good route to Waterloo Creek. All three streams are stocked only during the cool months. Patterson and Silver are pasture streams that would be hard to tell apart if you were dropped blindfolded at one or the other. Like all such streams, look for holdover fish at the sharp bends and other places where there might be fast water. Pine Creek flows through a lightly wooded area, the holes are quite a distance apart, and the stream in general requires some walking. Begin fishing at the beaver dam upstream from the parking lot (walk up the stocking road).

All three streams have a loyal following, with Pine being the most popular and Silver drawing the least fly-fishing attention, due, I suspect, to its proximity to French Creek.

FINDING SILVER CREEK

You can reach the south end of the designated portion of Silver Creek from Hanover Drive, which intersects Route 76 to the west. To reach the north end, follow Hanover east to County Road X20, called Lycurgus Road, turn left (north), and in a very short distance you'll find Sunflower Drive, which goes back west, downhill to the creek.

It's handy to know the route between Silver Creek and French Creek. From either end of Silver (i.e. either Hanover or Sunflower) go east, uphill to X20, and turn north (left) a short distance to Ebner Drive. Turn right onto Ebner and continue until you meet French Creek Road, where you should turn left.

From French Creek the directions are simply reversed:

Leave the upper parking and camping area at French Creek and follow French Creek Road south to Ebner, turn right and follow Ebner to X20 (Lycurgus Road), and turn left to reach either Sunflower or Hanover.

For a first visit to Silver Creek, I recommend starting from Hanover Drive and following the creek downstream to the north.

FINDING PATTERSON CREEK

Patterson is west of Route 76. You can reach the north end of the stocked area by turning west from 76 onto Iverson Bridge Road. Follow Iverson past Sandpiper to Ellingson Bridge Drive, which you take left, downhill to Patterson Creek Drive and the stream. Alternately, you can reach the south end of the designated area by taking Patterson Creek Drive west from Route 76, just a little south of the Iverson Road intersection. The stream will be on your right. A short section of oxbows upstream from a small white bridge is designated for fishing. These oxbows mark the point where Patterson Creek flows into the pasture.

The Patterson Creek Drive intersection is just over three miles north of the Waukon city limits.

FINDING PINE CREEK

There is a nice parking area for Pine Creek on Balsam Road, which is also W60. This is the same road you take between North and South Bear and Waterloo Creek or French Creek. If you continue south on W60 you will reach Patterson. To get to W60 from Highlandville, take the Highlandville Road south out of town and turn left onto Big Canoe Road at the cemetery. The pavement ends just before you reach W60 (most of the signs now say Balsam). Turn right to find Pine Creek's parking area.

Decorah & the Upper Iowa River Basin

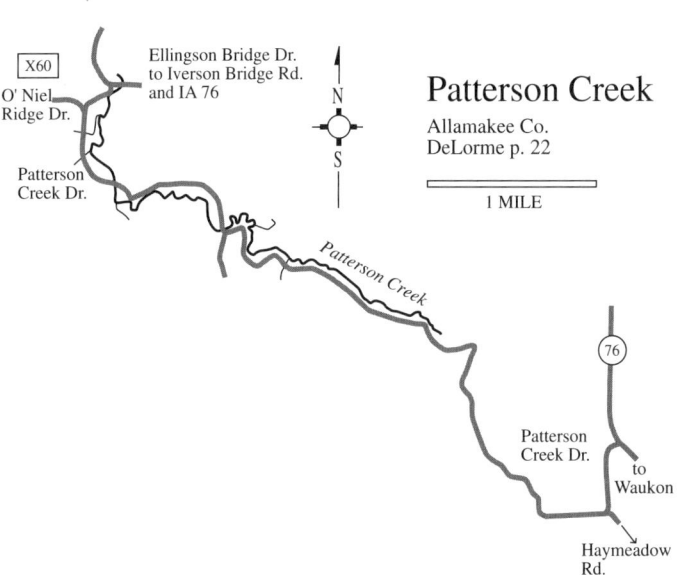

Pine Creek

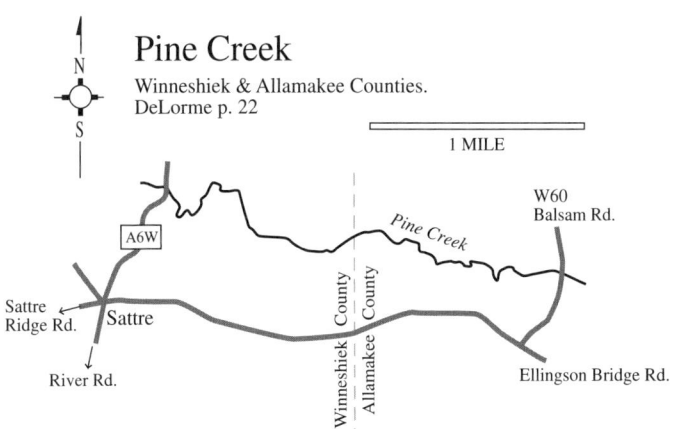

WEST CANOE CREEK

West Canoe, one of three streams northwest of Decorah, is an open and accessible pasture stream that snakes it way under a bridge on W34, which is easily found by taking U. S. 52 north from Decorah. Route W34 also bears the name North Winn Road. To reach the upper section of West Canoe, stay on Route 52 a bit longer and turn north (right) on 218th Avenue. Although West Canoe, like several other streams in this section, is a warm-water stream, don't hesitate to give it a try. As the popularity of fly fishing increases, some of these less-remarkable streams should provide good fishing opportunities, especially for beginners who will appreciate the favorable casting conditions afforded by pasture streams.

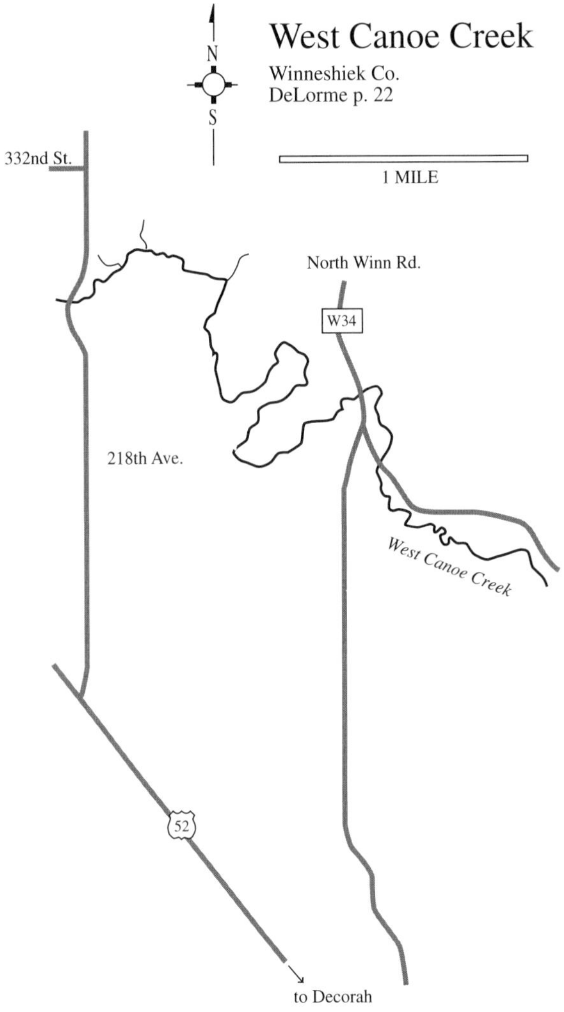
West Canoe Creek
Winneshiek Co.
DeLorme p. 22
N
S
1 MILE
332nd St.
North Winn Rd.
W34
218th Ave.
West Canoe Creek
52
to Decorah

Iowa Trout Streams

COLDWATER CREEK

Coldwater Creek has the most interesting headwaters of all the Iowa streams. Unfortunately, no one to my knowledge has ever seen them. The two miles or so that we fish between the Upper Iowa River and the stream's "source" are actually just a fraction of a waterway that flows for miles through a cave that is still being explored and mapped. The cave was discovered in the late 1960s by two spelunkers from the University of Iowa who used scuba equipment to reach the first room of the cave. Access now is by way of a 100-step ladder that descends through a shaft so narrow that you can let go of the ladder and lean back and rest if you want. Access is also restricted to people knowledgeable about caves. Visitors to the cave need wet suits in order to endure the water's 47°F temperature. This abundance of cold water not only gave the stream its name, it also accounts for Coldwater Creek's status as an excellent trout stream. Though a host of recreational activities, including fishing and canoeing the Upper Iowa River, attract many anglers to the stream, the runs between the obvious deep pools provide fly fishers with ample opportunity, regardless of how full the parking lot appears. This is one of the better streams in the state.

FINDING COLDWATER CREEK

If there is such a thing as a jinx, I've got one when it comes to finding this stream without getting lost either coming or going. Once, while trying a shortcut back to Cresco where I was staying, I found myself in Decorah. Here are a couple of the easier routes:

From the northwest corner of the Luther College campus in Decorah, go northwest on W20. As you leave town, you will cross the Upper Iowa River three time in rapid suc-

Decorah & the Upper Iowa River Basin

cession, and then there will be several miles before you see the river again. Don't turn off toward Cresco; instead, stay on W20, called Bluffton Road. When you do cross the river again, do not turn left or right, but continue straight, going up the hill in front of you. (This is not necessarily how it appears on the state's trout map.) Follow Bluffton Road northwest until you reach Coldwater Creek Road, which comes in from the left. It will take you directly to the stream. If you are in the neighborhood of Cresco, go north on Route 139, which looks like stair steps on the map as it makes its way through Kendallville, and then turn east on A18. Turn south on 278th Avenue and go back to the west when you reach Coldwater Creek Road.

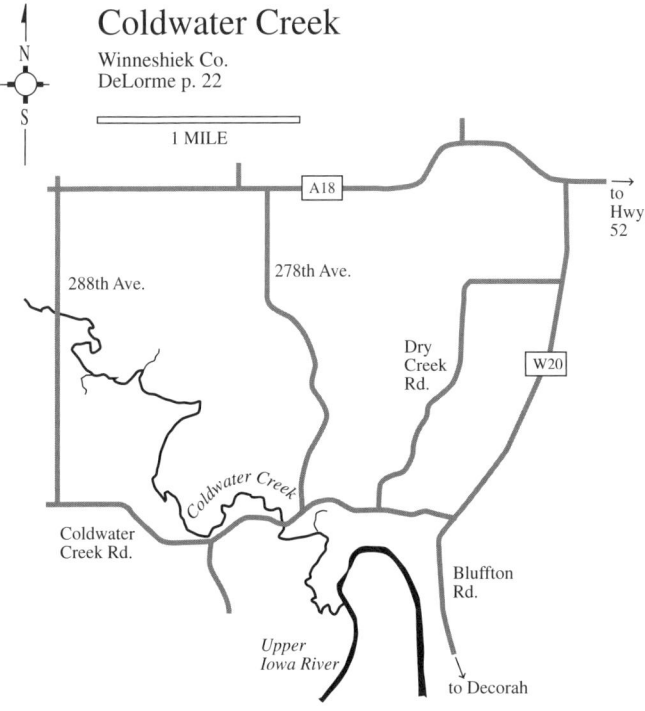

BIGALK

This little stretch of water (pronounced bee-yalk) would make an interesting side trip from Coldwater. The landowner has cooperated with several agencies to stabilize the banks and improve the waterway. You can reach Bigalk by taking 370th Street, which is the east-west road immediately north of A18. Take it west from Route 139. You will encounter the Upper Iowa River again, and as soon as the road crosses the river there is a fence crossing. A short jog at a stop sign puts you on 30th Street where there is another access to the stream.

Decorah & the Upper Iowa River Basin

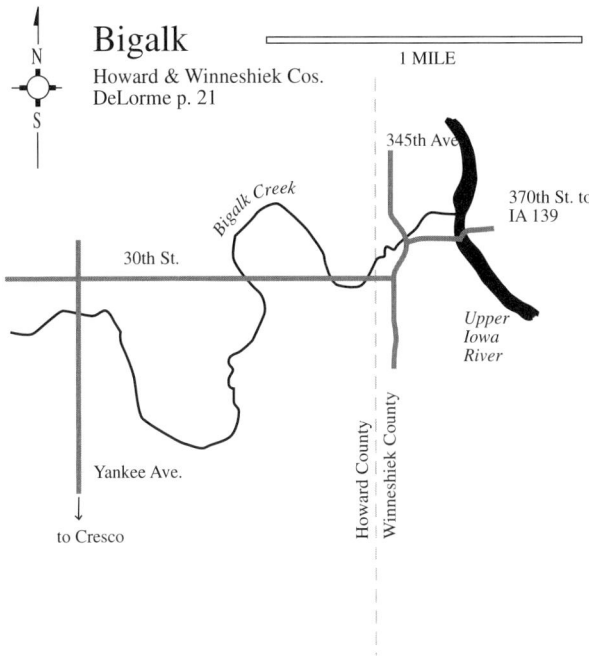

Iowa Trout Streams

BOHEMIAN CREEK

Though it doesn't flow into the Upper Iowa like the other streams in this chapter, this little creek is nevertheless closer to Decorah than it is to any other place I mention. If you have kinfolk around Protovin, you will already know about Bohemian. If you discover a long-lost in-law you need to visit in Protovin, take a lightweight rod along. From County Road B16 west of Spillville you should look for Ludwig Park and begin fishing there.

The most distinguishing feature of this short bit of stream is the road connecting it and Decorah—the Dvorak Highway. Hum a few bars of the New World Symphony as you drive along; this is the part of America that inspired it.

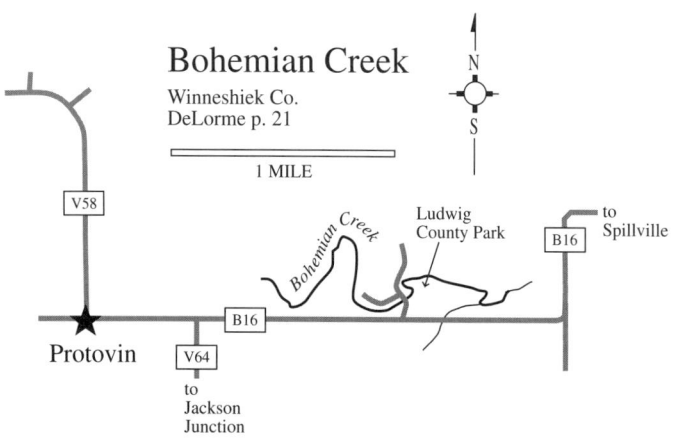

ALONG THE MISSISSIPPI

CLEAR CREEK • WEXFORD CREEK • PAINT CREEK • LITTLE PAINT CREEK • HICKORY CREEK • BLOODY RUN • SNY MAGILL • NORTH CEDAR • TURKEY RIVER (BIG SPRING) • BUCK CREEK • SOUTH CEDAR

Between the river towns of Lansing at the north and Guttenberg at the south are scattered ten streams, including some of the most popular among the general fishing public.

Also included in this section is the Turkey River, which is neither near the Mississippi nor, for than matter, a "trout stream." It appears here only because it is the site of the rearing station that stocks this area, and the river itself is stocked only for the sake of the facility's visitors. On the other hand, I never visit a trout facility without learning something worthwhile.

In this chapter, the streams are arranged as you would encounter them if you were driving south from Lansing.

123

CLEAR CREEK

There is some irony in the fact that the first stream on the DNR map, the stream bearing the number 1, is in my opinion the least consequential of them all. Clear Creek runs through a city park in Lansing, directly across Route 9 from the driveway to one of my regular haunts, the Scenic Valley Motel (the only motel in town). If you go to the park to let the kids play, that's fine, but the whole family could have a lot more fun at French Creek, less than ten minutes away.

The only access to the stream is across the road from the motel. If you look at the DNR map and assume that the road parallel to the creek will allow you to access the creek, you'll be wrong. The road is actually on the side of a high bluff looking down on the valley and the creek.

WEXFORD CREEK

This little stream has a small, but loyal, following, and I will admit to spending more time here than I ever plan. The creek is better proportioned to the roadside grotto than it is to the imposing church that overlooks it. The pool right at the bridge has some nice fish at times. And although Wexford Creek probably doesn't qualify as a destination, I certainly wouldn't drive past it unless I were in a hurry. It is a lovely little stream that meanders through pasture land on its short journey to the Mississippi.

Wexford Creek is located about seven miles south of Lansing at a bridge where X52 crosses the creek. You can't miss the church, cemetery, and tiny wayside chapel on the west side of the road, which is also the side where fence crossings have been built on both sides of the creek.

Along the Mississippi

Clear Creek
Allamakee Co.
DeLorme p. 23

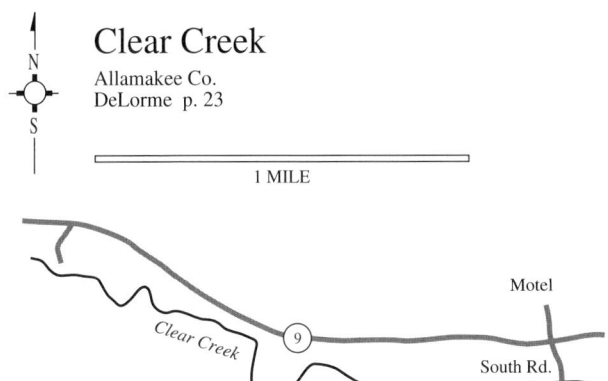

Wexford Creek
Allamakee Co.
DeLorme p. 23

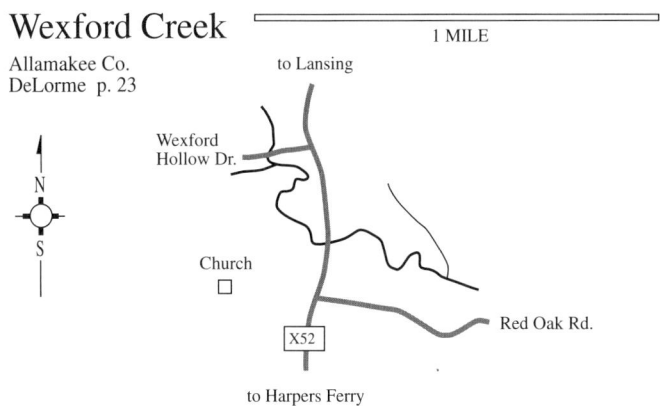

Iowa Trout Streams

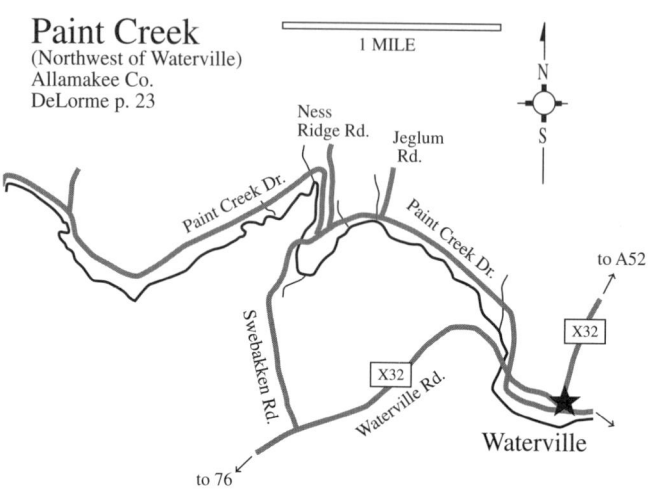

Paint Creek
(Northwest of Waterville)
Allamakee Co.
DeLorme p. 23

PAINT AND LITTLE PAINT CREEKS

As the map shows, Waterville is near the center of the designated waters of Paint Creek. If you have any doubts, take a look at the giant mural of a rainbow and jumping trout painted on the local tavern. The town of Waterville is convenient to vacationers camping in the Yellow River State Forest Reserve, and my guess is that these streams primarily are stocked for the park visitors. The section of Paint Creek west of Waterville is mostly pasture. You can see much of this stream from the road, and choose your fishing spots as you go along.

Little Paint, completely within the park, is very similar to Richmond Springs in Backbone State Park.

Along the Mississippi

FINDING PAINT AND LITTLE PAINT CREEKS

From Harpers Ferry, take X42 west to B25, then drive south into the park. To continue on to the sections of Paint Creek surrounding Waterville, turn right as you leave the south entrance to the park, and the creek will be on your left as you drive toward Waterville.

If you are approaching from State Highway 76, the western section of Paint Creek is reached by turning north on X32. The eastern portion and the entrance to the park are reached by turning north on B25.

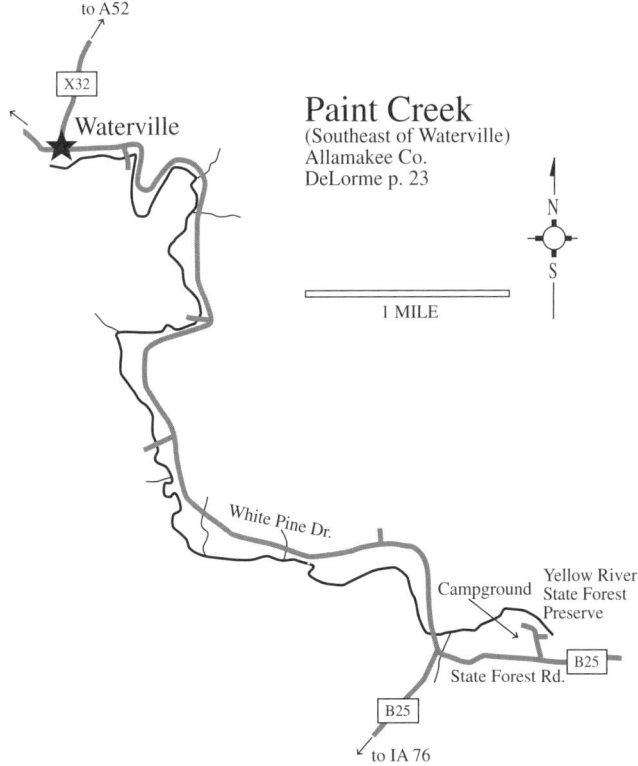

127

Iowa Trout Streams

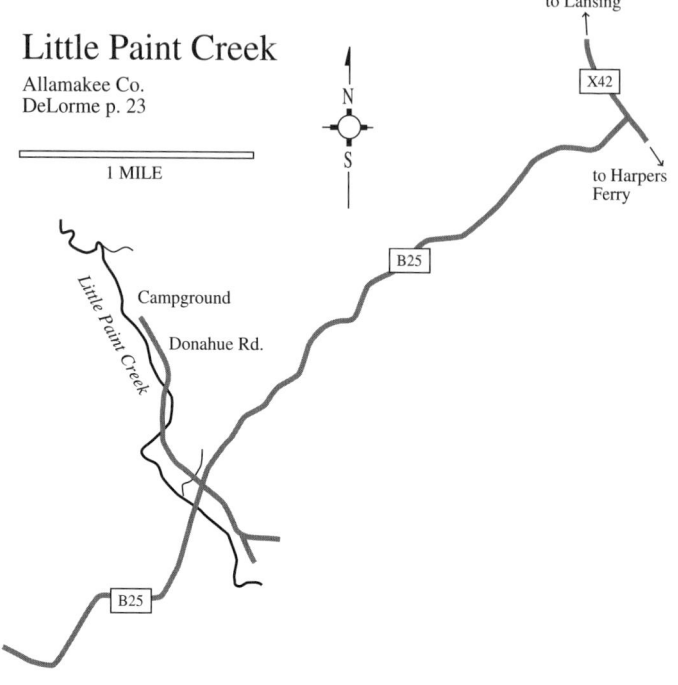

HICKORY CREEK

Hickory is farther from the Mississippi than the other streams in this chapter. It flows along the base of a steep hill and is separated from the road by a narrow strip of tilled fields. I don't recommend interpreting old, faded "Trout Water" signs as permission to go stomping through someone's corn or beans. In the absence of a stile and clearly defined path to the water, ask someone. For that matter, Hickory Creek intersects the road in two places, so you may as well invest your walking time in following the stream.

Along the Mississippi

I think it's significant to note that only brown trout and brook trout are stocked here, and that the stockings are not announced. This out-of-the-way stream could offer some interesting angling.

To reach Hickory Creek, follow County Road X26 north and, where it descends to cross the Yellow River, turn left onto Hickory Creek Road, which goes up, over, and along the ridge before dropping to the first bridge and stream access.

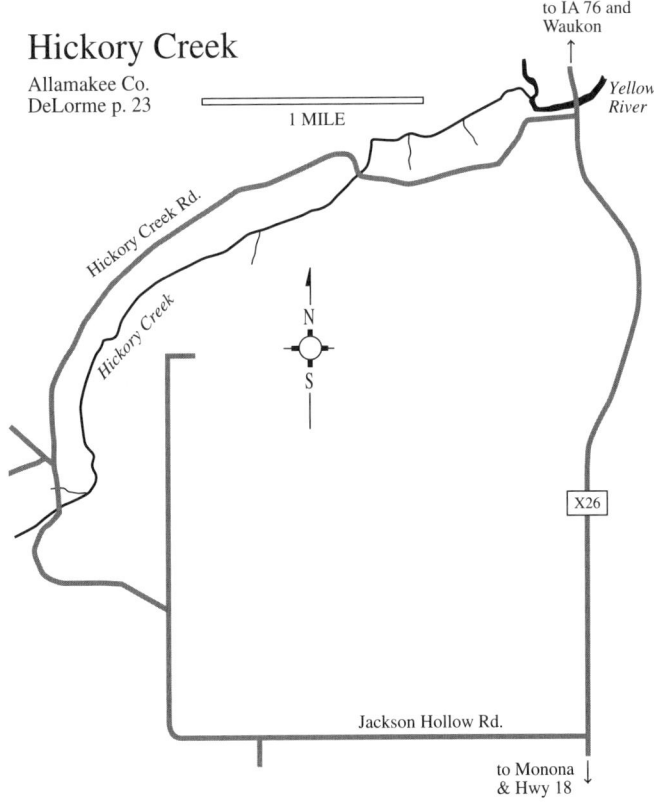

Iowa Trout Streams

BLOODY RUN

The next stream south along the Mississippi is Bloody Run, which has already been discussed on page 86, as one of the protected streams. Only a portion of the stream bears special regulations, however. The popular campground at the eastern end would certainly be a pleasant place to spend a few days.

SNY MAGILL AND NORTH CEDAR

Easy to find and to fish, with numerous parking spots, Sny Magill, like Big Mill discussed later, receives heavy pressure from the general angling public. There is, however, plenty of water to explore between stocking holes, and the stretch of North Cedar upstream from Sny Magill is less accessible and offers comparative solitude.

Sny Magill has been known to produce some exceptionally large browns. This is a stream where I would keep an eye on the insect activity and try woolly worms and streamers if the action is slow. Terrestrials, too, should be good producers. I recommend working the upstream portion first and immediately before dark checking the larger, downstream pools.

The future bodes well for Sny Magill and similar streams with silt problems. Agricultural management practices are being carefully studied and modified to reduce sediment in this and other Iowa streams.

FINDING SNY MAGILL AND NORTH CEDAR

From either U.S. 52 or State Highway 13 take B60, also called Ivory Road, to the east. Turn left on X50 (King Road) and directly in front of you will be a bridge with a parking area on the right.

Along the Mississippi

From MacGregor follow Business 18 out of town (away from the river) and watch for X50, which comes in from the left, and follow it to the stream.

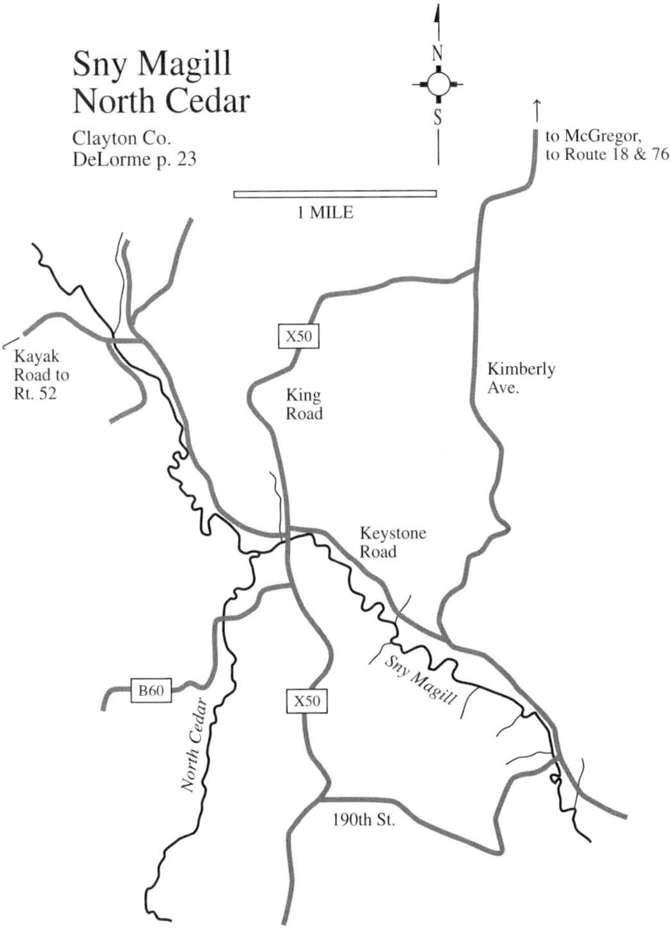

Sny Magill North Cedar

Clayton Co.
DeLorme p. 23

TURKEY RIVER (BIG SPRING)

The Turkey River is included in this section by default. Its relationship to any other stream is geographic only in the sense that the Big Spring rearing station provides fish to streams in a wide radius from here. If you are passing through Elkader, take a run out to the facility to look around, and while you are there, make a few casts. Trout in the river tend to congregate in the area where the cold water from the hatchery flows into the river.

FINDING TURKEY RIVER

First, admire the longest keystone arch bridge west of the Mississippi. It's on Bridge Street. Then find North High Street, which is on the north side of the river. That will take you to X16, which is also called Gunder Road. About five miles out of town you will reach Big Spring Road, where you take a left and go a similar distance to the rearing station. The waters in the campground where you first enter are sometimes stocked early in the season.

Across the river from the rearing station is a campground at Frieden Park, which you reach from Carter Street in Elkader (Carter turns into C1X as you leave town).

Along the Mississippi

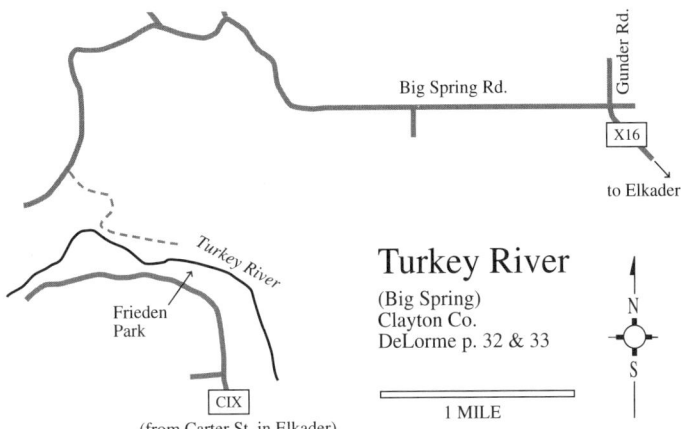

Turkey River
(Big Spring)
Clayton Co.
DeLorme p. 32 & 33

BUCK CREEK

Buck Creek is a good-size stream that takes some effort to explore. The upper access is a small county park, the middle access is the site of a beautiful old brick mill, and the lowest access is near a quarry. I recommend beginning first in the middle and exploring both up and down. After that you can fish from the ends; there is a good deal of decent water here, and no easy approaches. Though Buck Creek isn't stocked in warm weather, its length and size are a good indication that you should expect to find fish here almost anytime, if you cover some water.

FINDING BUCK CREEK

The upper portion of Buck Creek is reached from County Road C17 (Van Buren), which runs between Garnavillo and X56, the road that follows the Mississippi. The little park is at the bottom of a steep drive that appears almost immediately after you turn left from C17.

The middle section is reached by continuing straight at the point where Buck Creek Road curves to the right. It is a fair weather road.

The lowest access has parking on the north side, before you cross the bridge.

Along the Mississippi

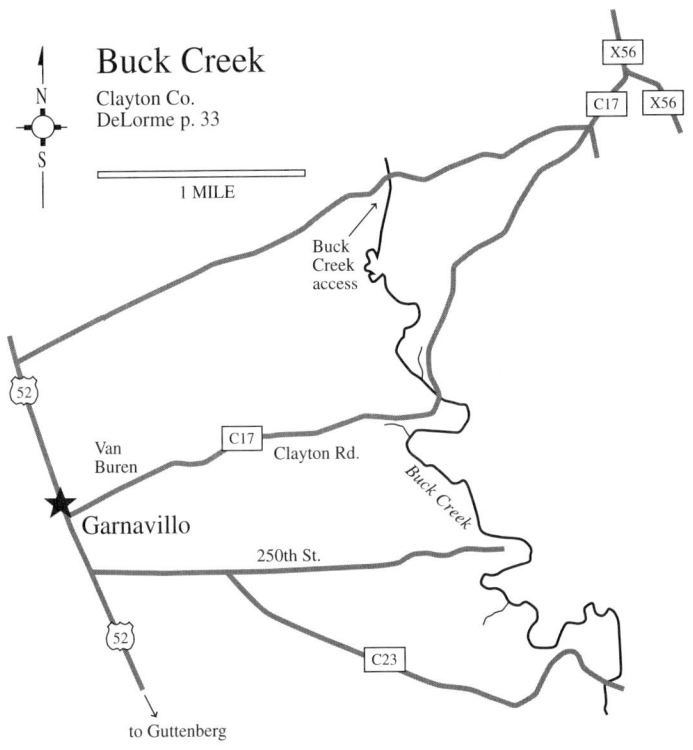

 *Iowa Trout Streams*

SOUTH CEDAR CREEK

South Cedar Creek, just outside Garnavillo, is a pleasant, easy-to-fish stream that skirts a steep wooded hillside and flows through pasture land. Though not cold enough to be stocked during the summer, this is nonetheless a nice place to fish.

On the DNR map it appears that you can reach the upstream end by going west out of town, but the best approach is to go south on Highway 52 and turn onto Jigsaw road. Park and fish upstream from the bridge, staying to the left where the stream forks.

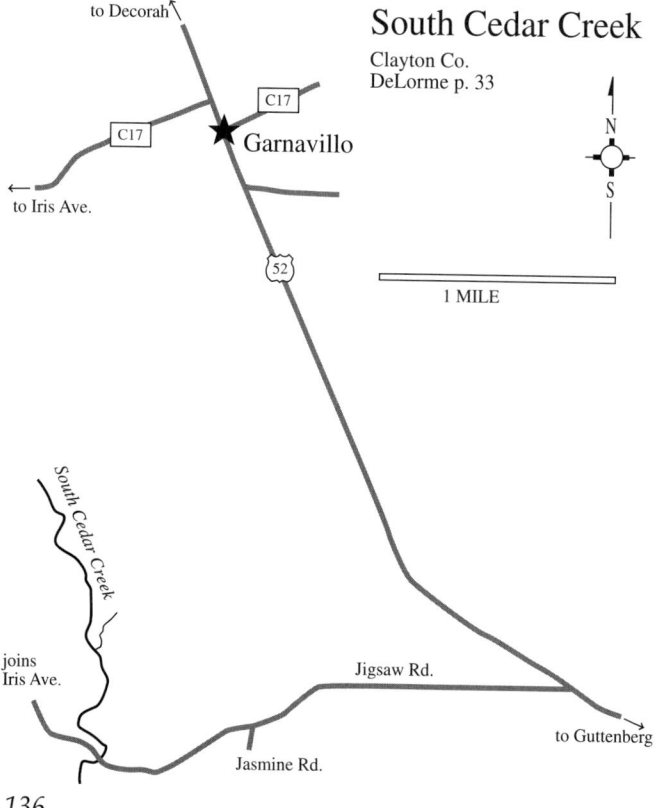

FAYETTE COUNTY

OTTER CREEK • GLOVERS CREEK • GRANNIS CREEK • BEAR CREEK • MINK CREEK

Around the towns of West Union and Fayette are five streams that are popular with local anglers. All are worth some attention if you are passing through the area. Grannis and Glovers are both coldwater streams, but because Glovers is so heavily fished, my recommendation is that Grannis is your best bet for a short outing. If simply being outdoors is as valuable to you as the quantity of fish you catch, the hike to and along Bear Creek should be a worthwhile excursion.

OTTER CREEK AND GLOVERS CREEK

Although these two streams join, they are seldom fished on the same outing. The confluence of the two streams, located a substantial distance from any road access, is one of the many spots I hope to explore someday. Glovers is a lovely, small pasture stream that supports some fish through the winter. There is one run through the pasture that has abundant watercress, which translates to abundant cover where trout can avoid anglers when the pressure is on. This, like so many places, would be one to check out in the final moments of daylight.

Otter Creek, on the other hand, is a hefty piece of water that has a little bit of everything. The trout waters start at the dramatic cliffs in Echo Valley State Park and run more than nine miles to the town of Elgin. Consult the state trout map and look for stiles to be sure any given section is open to angling.

When you enter Echo Valley, it is the water to your left that holds fish. From Elgin back upstream, the creek follows Echo Valley Road, then crosses under it at an old steel bridge and disappears to the north. The next access is reached by following the road and turning right on Hornet Road, which descends to a concrete bridge that crosses Otter. Fish both up and down from here. Here, as on many streams, I recommend first trying dry flies on the upper, faster waters, then streamers and wooly worms on the slower, deeper sections.

FINDING OTTER AND GLOVERS

To reach Echo Valley Road and the park from West Union, proceed east (toward town) on State Highway 18 from its intersection with State Highway 150. At the second traffic signal, just past the ball field, turn right onto Pine Street

Fayette County

(Pine Street to the left is County Road W42). Follow Pine downhill and bear left at the foot of the hill where there is an apartment building on the right. This is Echo Valley Road, and the entrance to the park is on the left, 1.7 miles ahead. Immediately upon turning you can either turn left again to reach the parking area at Glovers, or take the right fork down into the park. If you do not enter the park, Echo Valley Road becomes gravel and proceeds past Hornet Road and on to Elgin.

The other route you need to know is the one from West Union to the concrete bridge on Hornet described above. For this route you continue east through town on 18 and turn right on B64 (Golden Road) at the point where 18 curves northeastward. Take the first right turn onto Hazel Road, and it will take you to the concrete bridge where Hornet and Hazel Roads meet.

In Elgin, which is connected to West Union by both Echo Valley Road and Golden Road (B64), the bridge over Otter Creek is just south of the water tower. If you follow Echo Valley Road along the stream and continue straight instead of turning on Hornet Road as described above, you will reach the entrance to the park (now on your right), just where the gravel turns to pavement.

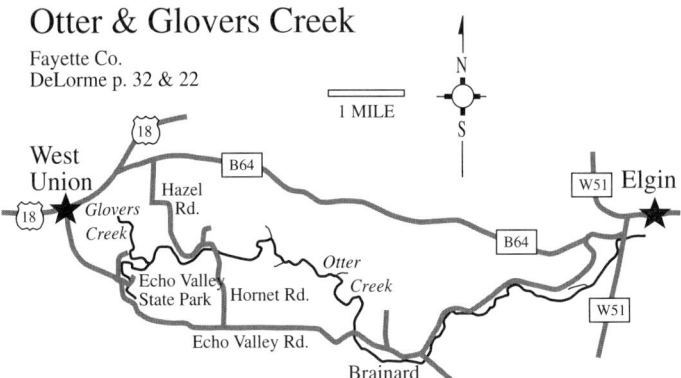

139

Iowa Trout Streams

GRANNIS CREEK AND BEAR CREEK

Grannis is a coldwater stream that flows through wooded land surrounded by steep hills. It holds fish throughout the year and is easy to find. Bear flows through similar country, but is a larger stream and not stocked during the summer. Grannis affords the easiest access, while Bear Creek, on the other side of a ridge that separates the two, offers solitude because of the walking required to reach it.

FINDING GRANNIS AND BEAR

Access to these streams is from C24, also called Kornhill Road, which follows the ridge between the streams and connects Fayette to the town of Wadena.

If you are looking at the state trout map and trying to find Bear, beware: a road branching off from W51 south of Wadena appears to lead directly to the western end of the stocked area, but while it begins as a road (Delta Road), it soon deteriorates into a steep, high-risk trail usable only in ideal conditions with four-wheel drive. The best approach is from 128th Street at C24.

The approach to the center section of Grannis is about a hundred yards away on the opposite side of C24, clearly labeled Grannis Road.

An alternate route to Grannis, one that will take you to a parking area at the confluence with the Volga River, begins in Wadena by taking East Harriman, which becomes Derby Road shortly before you turn left onto Depot Road. Follow Depot Road to Fox Road, turn left to cross the Volga, and park at the parking area.

Grannis Creek

Fayette Co.
DeLorme p. 32

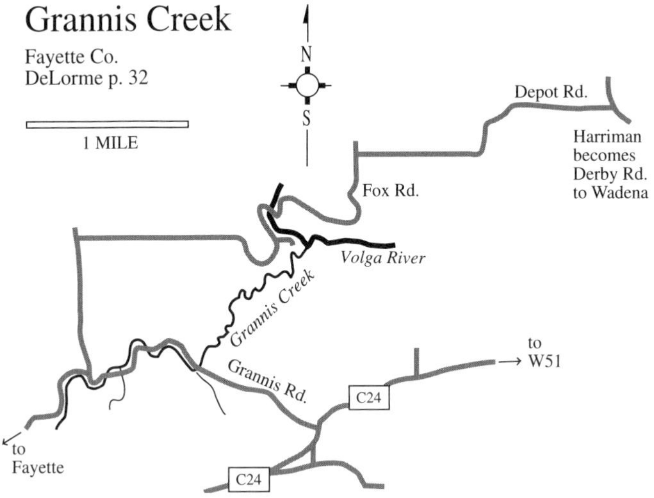

Bear Creek

Fayette Co.
DeLorme p. 32

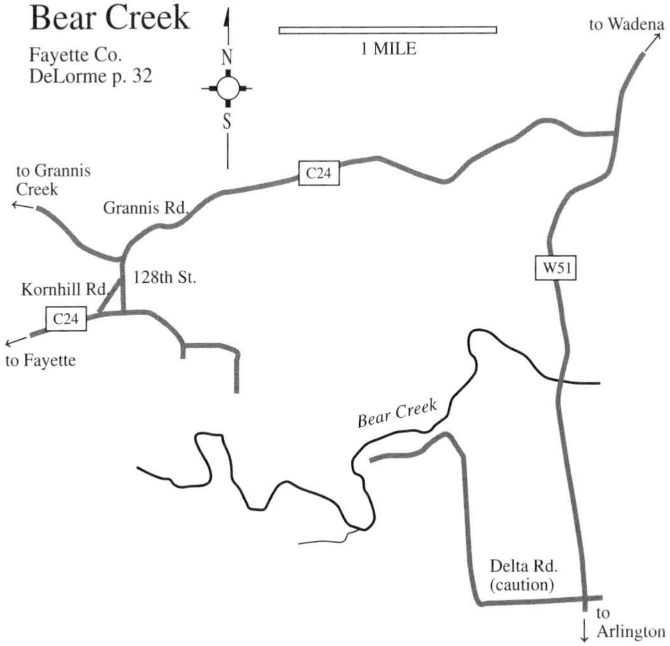

Iowa Trout Streams

MINK CREEK

Mink is a relatively slow-moving stream that is not stocked in warm weather. There is a substantial length of it, however, that can only be reached on foot and should hold carry-over trout. If I were in the area for a time, I would make a project of fishing the section of it that runs between Bear Road and Bighorn Road.

Mink runs along W51, Cedar Road, north of Wadena and south of Highway 56 (Fillmore Road). A section not shown on my map lies west of W51 and is reached from Highway 56 by taking Dogwood Road to the south.

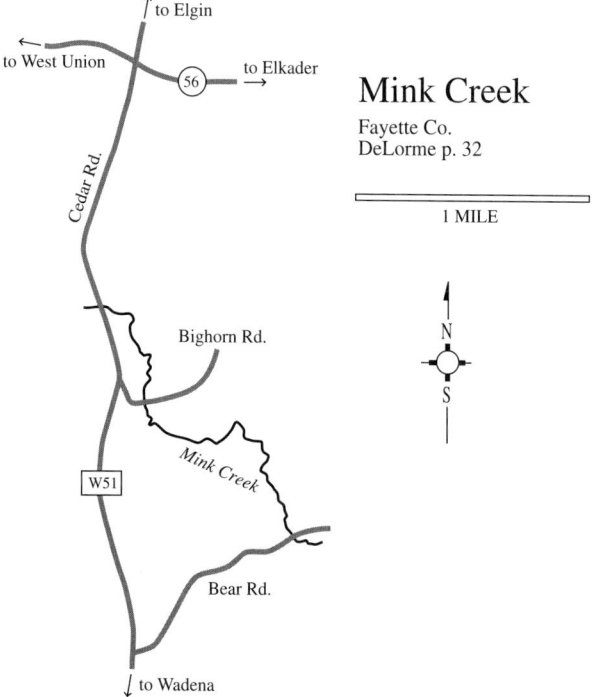

Mink Creek
Fayette Co.
DeLorme p. 32

The Backbone Area & East

Richmond Springs • Joy Springs • Maquoketa River • Little Turkey River • Fountain Springs • Twin Bridges • Bankston (Middle Fork of the Little Maquoketa)

Backbone State Park, one of the most striking scenic areas in the state, can be the focal point of fine angling and a relaxing family vacation. This area is also reasonably close to Manchester and Spring Branch Creek, and as you travel east along Route 3 there are several parks with trout-stream access.

Richmond Springs

Richmond Springs, the best-known of the three streams included here, has excellent numbers of trout. During the winter, when the park is closed, the stream still can be reached on foot, and large numbers of resident rainbows have been caught in the off season. I recommend releasing winter rainbows to perpetuate the quality of this off-season fishery. The park's managers may modify the season somewhat depending on the weather, but figure that the park roads close on November 15 and reopen on April 15. The walk from the north entrance to the upper reaches of the stream is about one-half mile.

Richmond Springs trout seem to have a healthy appetite for wooly worm patterns, black in particular. The wooly worm is always an effective trout pattern, especially when tied as small as a #14; but in this stream, the larger sizes seem to work well.

FINDING RICHMOND SPRINGS

Backbone State Park has four main entrances, and it is the North Gate that is closest to Richmond Springs. To get to the North Gate, use State Highway 410, which begins at the intersection of State Highways 3 and 13 outside Strawberry Point. From that intersection, 410 goes west for one mile and then curves south into the North Gate, which is on 400th Street.

Once inside the park, you'll see the stream on your right as you descend to the bridge and first picnic area. After following the road and passing under it several times, Richmond Springs goes off to the right. There is a long stretch of stream, from where it veers away from the road to its confluence with the Maquoketa River, that can be reached only on foot.

When you approach from the West Gate and descend the hill, you must turn left past the shelters, and follow that road to Balanced Rock, which is directly over one of Richmond Springs' popular pools (popular in normal or wet seasons, I should say). From the West Gate, the first water you see is the Maquoketa River, not Richmond Springs. The Maquoketa also is a designated trout stream, but its best fishing water is above the park. If you fail to make the left turn toward Richmond Springs, the road crosses the Maquoketa just past a sign indicating "Trout Waters." Don't let this sign confuse you. Richmond Springs is about a mile away.

On the eastern side of the park there are two entrances, both clearly marked as you go north on County Road W69.

The Backbone Area & East

It is the one farthest north, the East Gate off Route C57, that you want. (C57 intersects W69 from the west.) From this entrance, proceed past the park office to the Maquoketa River crossing described above. At the park office, you can pick up a free map that will help you find your way through the park.

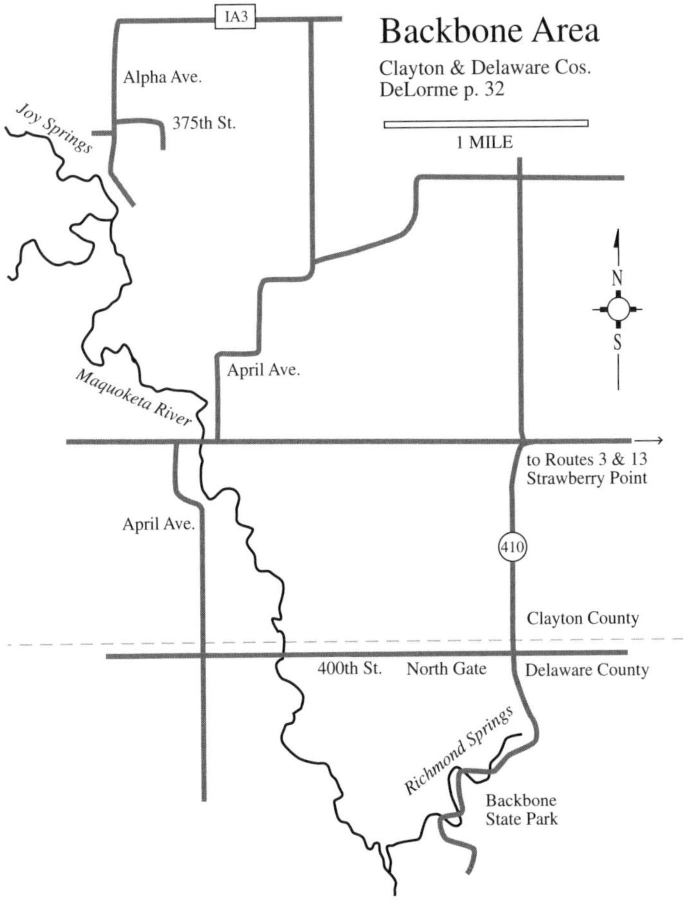

Backbone Area
Clayton & Delaware Cos.
DeLorme p. 32

JOY SPRINGS AND THE MAQUOKETA

Joy Springs is not a stream, but the name of the park where trout stocking begins on the Maquoketa River. Joy Springs is a great little park with decent waters, though not a lot of good holding water. I would consider it the first or last stop in a day of fishing the entire length of the river between there and Backbone (or close to it).

Downstream from Joy Springs are two other access points to the Maquoketa River, both of them bridges, and both of them have fishable areas either upstream or downstream. There is potentially good fishing here that is sometimes overlooked by anglers crowding into the park.

Joy Springs is a well-marked turnoff from State Highway 3, just west of Strawberry Point. The remainder of the Maquoketa is accessed from the bridges mentioned above, the lower of which is due west of the North Gate of the park.

LITTLE TURKEY

The fishable section of the Little Turkey flows through a state-owned wildlife area and has a number of things to recommend it. The trout stockings include fingerlings along with adult fish, the stockings are not announced, and the terrain and location are such that it probably isn't worth the effort for anglers who lay-in-wait for the stocking truck. The stabilized banks where the state land begins make a good starting point for an upstream excursion. While its population of fish might not match that of some of the better-known streams, the Little Turkey probably receives less fishing pressure.

The Backbone Area & East

FINDING LITTLE TURKEY

Finding this stream is a cinch once you find the road out of the nearest town, Colesburg. After you enter town from the south, past a sign that announces Colesburg as the "Gateway to the Beautiful Hill Country," you will come to a four-way stop at First Street. Turn right (east), and then turn right once again, either on Franklin or a block farther at the school. This will leave you heading south, just a short block from Hubbard Street, which you should take east out of town. Hubbard Street becomes Voyager Road as you go east. At the bottom of a hill, look for 329th Avenue and a sign indicating the Little Turkey. An old county road leads to a parking area.

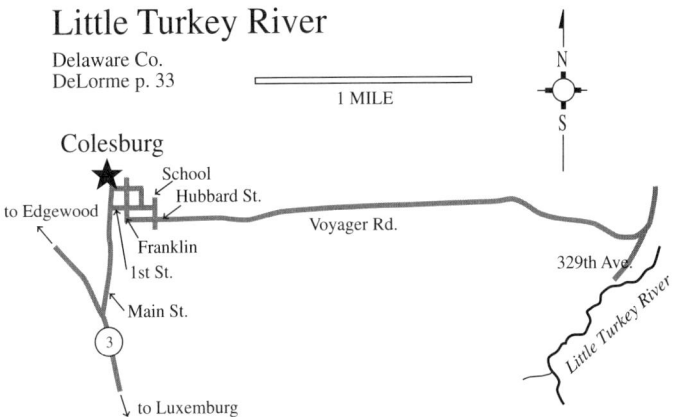

147

Iowa Trout Streams

FOUNTAIN SPRINGS AND TWIN BRIDGES

These two park streams are fished heavily by the general public; you may have to work—and be lucky—to find holdover fish. Twin Bridges Park, on Elk Creek, is developed and has an almost carnival feel to it, while Fountain Springs, just a couple of minutes away, seems wilder and, except on stocking days, is rather peaceful—a pretty and quiet place for a siesta and some leisurely casting on weekday afternoons.

Fountain Springs is a short creek that is joined by another spring creek, Odell Branch, before it merges with Elk Creek just downstream from Twin Bridges park. The area is geologically interesting because of the spring heads, and it offers fuel for speculation about what the fish population of these tiny creeks might have been like in pioneer days.

At Twin Bridges, there is parking at the western end, and from there you can fish downstream into a hiking and wildlife area, and away from the playground and picnic area.

Twin Bridges is located on Route 3, where the highway crosses Elk Creek east of Backbone State Park. On the eastern side of Twin Bridges is an intersection with 265th Avenue. At the western end of the park is Rainbow Road, which leads to Oak Road and Fountain Springs.

The Backbone Area & East

Twin Bridges & Fountain Springs
Delaware Co.
DeLorme p. 33

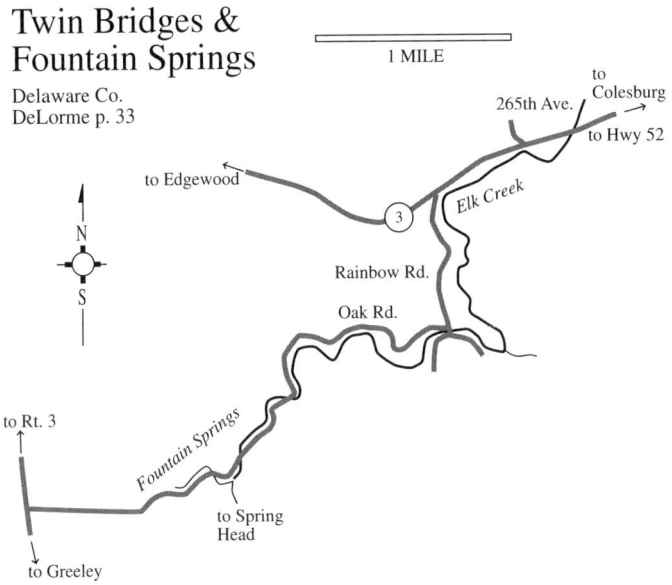

BANKSTON (MIDDLE FORK OF THE LITTLE MAQUOKETA)

Unlike Twin Bridges Park, this quiet little park beside the stream is little more than a place to stop and have a picnic. The stream itself is a genuine coldwater creek (the Middle Fork of the Little Maquoketa), and you may find some resident trout a considerable distance downstream from the highway.

The easiest way to find the stream is to take County Road Y17, or Bankston Park Road, south from Route 3. To approach the park from the south (i.e. Route 20), first find the town of Bankston, which is distinguished, like many little towns in the area, by a convincingly inspirational church steeple. Bankston is situated on County Road Y17, almost due north of Epworth, which makes it northeast of Dyersville (in case you need a motel or want to visit baseball's Field of Dreams). Route Y17 is also called Bankston Park Road from this direction; and from either direction you go downhill as you near the park and stream.

The Backbone Area & East

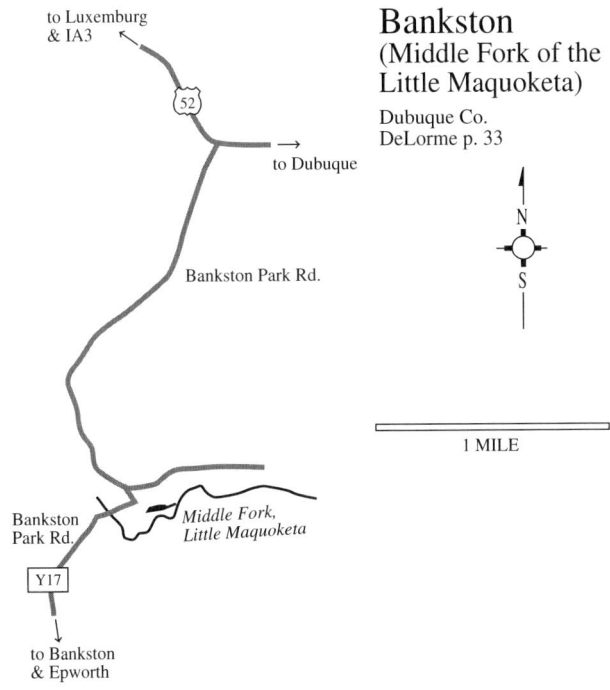

Iowa Trout Streams

An old iron bridge and fisherman's stile typical of Iowa's trout region.

SWISS VALLEY & THE SOUTHERN STREAMS

UPPER AND LOWER SWISS VALLEY • BIG MILL CREEK • LITTLE MILL CREEK • BRUSH CREEK

Only four trout streams are found south of U.S. 20. Upper and Lower Swiss Valley (Catfish Creek), while not right on the highway like Spring Branch, is still less than five minutes from U.S. 20. About 45 minutes farther south are the three streams I call the "southern" streams—Big Mill, Little Mill, and Brush Creek.

UPPER AND LOWER SWISS VALLEY (CATFISH CREEK)

This easy-to-find stream, which on the state's map is identified as "Upper and Lower Swiss Valley," is long enough to provide a variety of trout habitat, and it is served by a large modern campground, a nice park, and a nature center with displays, restrooms, and hiking trails. Swiss Valley offers a nice blend of fishing and family vacationing. The area is lovely and interesting, and the fishing is quite respectable.

Upstream from the nature center, the upper reaches of the stream (Catfish Creek) were protected by special regulations for a couple of seasons, and may hold good-sized fish. Large fish have also been recorded from the lower section at the campground. I've caught nice fish from the middle portion simply by prospecting with an Orange Governor, one of the classic wet flies I tie. Terrestrials produce well here in the summer months. The official designation of Upper Swiss begins where the service road above the nature center crosses the stream. It is upstream from there that fly anglers can expect the best action. The extreme upper end flows from the grounds of a beautiful monastery, but I recommend reaching it by road.

FINDING SWISS VALLEY

Following U.S. 20 from the west, Swiss Valley is about 33 miles from Manchester. Well-marked with brown and yellow signs directing you to Swiss Valley, the road, Swiss Valley Road, turns off of Route 20 to the right as you reach the outskirts of Dubuque where 20 bends northeast toward Dubuque proper. Alternately, the other end of this road is reached from U.S. 151 as it leaves Dubuque. From Dubuque, follow 151 about 2.5 miles from the very edge of town, until you reach an interchange where U.S. 61 continues to the left. You must exit to the right to stay on 151. A mile and a half

Swiss Valley & The Southern Streams

farther on is a brown-and-white Conservation Commission sign indicating the right turn toward Swiss Valley. This is Military Road, and about a mile farther on another sign will direct you to the left onto Swiss Valley Road. From this direction you reach the turnoff to the campground first, followed by the park at the bridge and then the nature center.

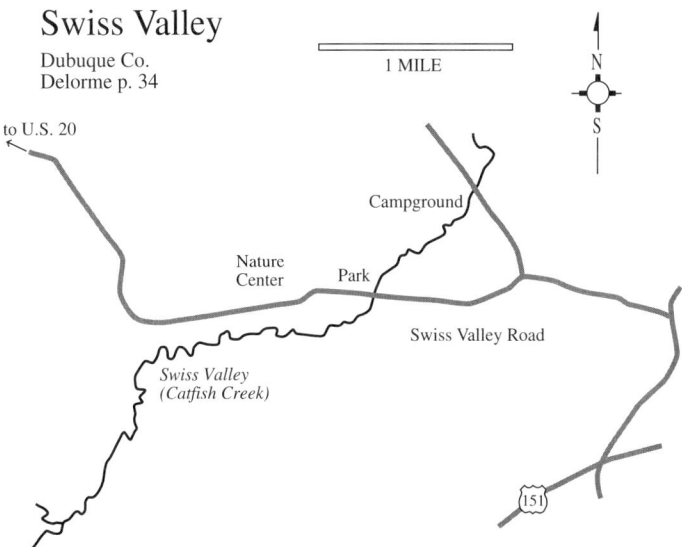

Iowa Trout Streams

THE SOUTHERN STREAMS

Of the three streams off to themselves at the southern extreme of trout country, Big and Little Mill Creeks and Brush Creek, each is unique and has a different kind of appeal.

BIG MILL CREEK

Big Mill, stocked with all three trout species, is indeed the larger of the two creeks by that name. Big Mill and Little Mill converge just after they pass under State Highway 62, and just before they fall into the Mississippi River. The fact that it is the larger simply means that Big Mill has longer, wider pools, and from a fly-fishing point of view that simply means greater popularity with bait fishers. Bear in mind that these streams are the ones closest to the numerous anglers from the Davenport area (the "Quad Cities").

The advice I've already given on dealing with fishing pressure remains true here: Look for fish between the stocking holes. Even on the most crowded Saturday morning, I have found rising fish (and comparative solitude) by looking for fast, narrow runs or deep riffles between the pools. When you do find a fish in this situation, take your time and enjoy working it. If necessary, change flies often, seine the water for insect samples, rest the spot frequently, and study what the rises look like.

The stream bottom in the big pools is clay and can be very slippery. I recommend lug-soled wading shoes rather than felt-soled ones if you are going to wade that type of pool. In large, slow pools you need to wade slowly and carefully to avoid sending waves of muddy water ahead of you.

The portion of Big Mill that is stocked is relatively short, and the two parking areas are only one-half mile apart.

Swiss Valley & The Southern Streams

These parking areas also provide access to public land for hunters and hikers and such, so all the cars you see won't necessarily belong to anglers. The best fly-fishing water is behind the marsh and upstream a little.

FINDING BIG MILL CREEK

If you are traveling on Route 62, which is State Street in Bellevue, turn north (left when driving toward the Mississippi) on Seventh Street, and in a couple of blocks you will find a five-way stop. Take the road that bears left (not the hard left) and you will be on Mill Creek Road. This is the road you want, but be careful to stay on it. The road forks almost immediately, with paved road curving uphill to the right, while the road you want changes abruptly to gravel and is marked D57. You want to go straight on the gravel for 4.3 miles.

No matter how hard you try, you will miss the first parking area for the simple reason that the drive is invisible until you are past it. Once you have passed it you should see the parking area on your left and go back. Otherwise, you'll almost immediately see the Big Mill Homestead maintained by the local historical society.

Beyond the historical society building there is a marsh and then the second parking area, which is almost exactly one-half mile from the first.

If you are traveling on U.S. 52 through Bellevue, D57 butts right into it. D57 is also called Park Street. Route 52 occupies the place where First Street should be, but apparently "Riverview" sounds better. So U.S. 52 is Riverview, and Second, Third, etc. run parallel to it. Don't worry; you can't get lost in Bellevue anyway.

There is a motel on the northern outskirts of town, and there is the Riverview Hotel (Saloon-Rooms-Food) right at the junction of State (Rt. 62) and Riverview (Rt. 52). It has loads of character, including truly classy rooms, some of

157

Iowa Trout Streams

which allow you to watch the sun rise over Lock and Dam No. 12 on the Mississippi River. Antique furniture, complete with real crocheted doilies under porcelain dishes holding herbs and stuff make it resemble a bed-and-breakfast, but less costly and with a down-home cafe and lively bar downstairs.

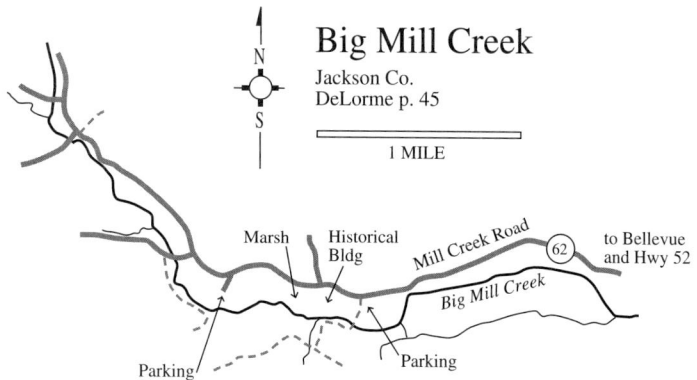

Swiss Valley & The Southern Streams

LITTLE MILL CREEK

This narrower twin of Big Mill runs a little faster, which means a couple of things. First, there seems to be less sediment, and second, there are more places for trout to hang out. The DNR apparently agrees, because the stream has benefited from some habitat improvement and is stocked primarily with brown trout. Although the two streams are accessed via different roads, it is still easy to get from one to the other. For fly fishing, though, I like Little Mill much better. If I were stopping over in the area with only limited fishing time, this would be my choice over Big Mill or Brush Creek.

Like all of the diminutive streams, it's easy to frighten the fish before getting a chance to cast to them. I have spooked fish here by failing to see them in the riffles immediately below pools. By "immediately," I mean their noses were right in the chute of water cascading from what to them must have been an otherwise boring pool. Always be wary when approaching pools from downstream. Often there will be a fish or two in the first couple of feet of riffle below the pool. With a standard-length leader, you should be able to put your fly a couple of feet into the pool and still have the butt of it behind the fish. Be ready. The water moves fast at the tail, and the fish must strike quickly to get your offering.

The pools here are smaller and not as likely to get pressured by bait anglers. Little Mill is my current favorite of the Southern streams.

FINDING LITTLE MILL

There is a description of the Bellevue street layout and the town's amenities above. Little Mill is accessed from D61, called Bellevue-Cascade Road, which butts into State Highway 62 (State Street) at the edge of town, just west of

Iowa Trout Streams

the school. (Because everything in town runs parallel to the river, northbound streets actually run northwest, and the westbound streets perpendicular to them run southwest.) Follow Bellevue-Cascade Road 1.6 miles and turn left onto the gravel road, 216th Street, which runs through the same valley as the stream. There is a stone house at the intersection, and you can take another left almost immediately and stop at the first parking area, or you can proceed another 1.3 miles and find a couple of stiles that will take you over the fence and through the pasture to the stream.

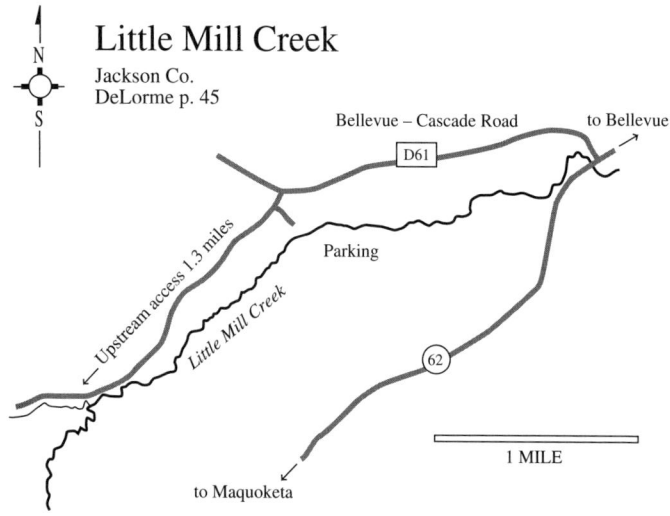

Swiss Valley & The Southern Streams

BRUSH CREEK

Brush Creek, the southernmost of all the Iowa trout streams, is characterized by long slow pools meandering through pasture land. Most of what I've said about Big Mill is applicable to Brush.

Although there doesn't appear to be a great deal of good holding water, I have seen brown trout going through their mating antics here. It's doubtful that the neighborhood is the greatest for raising a family, but I know that those particular fish eluded capture for a while. The stream probably sustains a few resident fish, and the location is lovely. While not a stream to stake your hopes on for a serious fly-fishing adventure, it would be an excellent place to teach kids or friends how to fish. And for that, I would be tempted to be there on stocking day.

On the map, it looks as though two roads out of Andrew lead to the stream. In fact, one of them deteriorates into a Level B Service road. To get to the creek easily, follow State Highway 62 northerly through Andrew and take the first right on the gravel road marked 154th Street. Turn left when it butts into another gravel road, 261st Avenue, and as it winds downhill the old steel bridge at the base of an impressive limestone cliff will come into view. Park at the crossover there and fish the designated waters downstream.

On the map you will also see a short section of the creek upstream from here. To get there, proceed across the bridge and follow the road until it meets 298th Avenue, where you turn left to return to Route 62. Turn right, away from Andrew, and go one-half mile to 200th Street (it's right next to a house, so don't overlook it thinking it is a driveway). Follow 200th; it will cross a bridge, and the stream will be on your left, marked by crossovers.

Iowa Trout Streams

Brush Creek
Jackson Co.
DeLorme p. 45

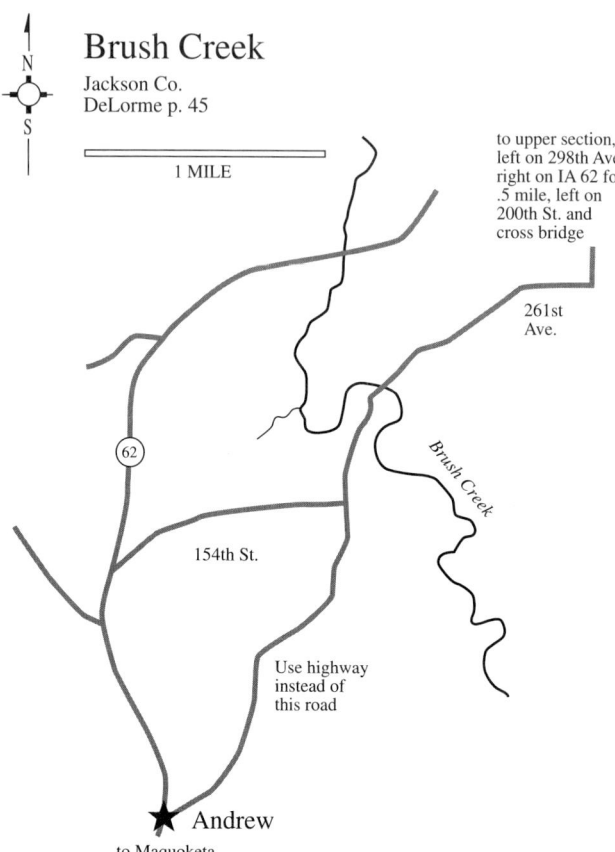

The Trout Country Panhandle

Spring Creek • Turtle Creek • Wapsi (Wapsipinicon) River

Almost completely isolated from the rest of Iowa's trout streams are three warm-water streams in Mitchell County, in the vicinity of Mason City. Popular among business travelers who have to make stops in the state's major northern city, these streams often provide respectable fishing. The only reported problem I've heard is from an angler who had a fish on when the boss rang in on the cell phone in his vest.

Iowa Trout Streams

SPRING CREEK

Spring Creek, perhaps the least promising of the Panhandle streams, flows through the little town of Orchard, which is most easily found by taking Route 218 south from Route 9, the main east-west highway through northern Iowa. Four miles south of Route 9, turn west on 320th Street. That will be Orchard Drive, and once in town you will find access to the stream by turning north on either T42 or onto March Avenue.

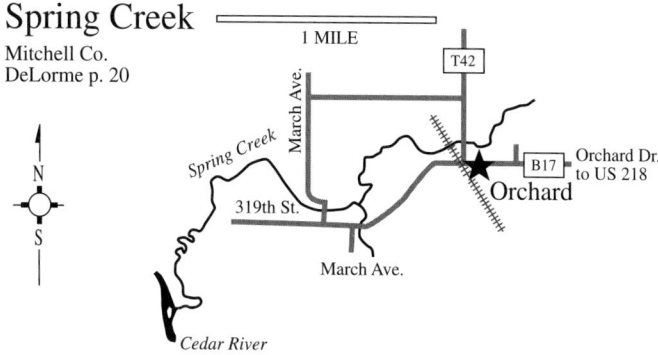

The Trout Country Panhandle

TURTLE CREEK

Although there is an access to Turtle Creek on U. S. 218 near the railroad tracks at the north edge of St. Ansgar, the water there moves so slowly at times you can't tell which way the creek is flowing. A better access place is found by continuing north on the highway until you reach 440th Street, where you turn right. After about a mile, you will find a stile where the stream flows under the road.

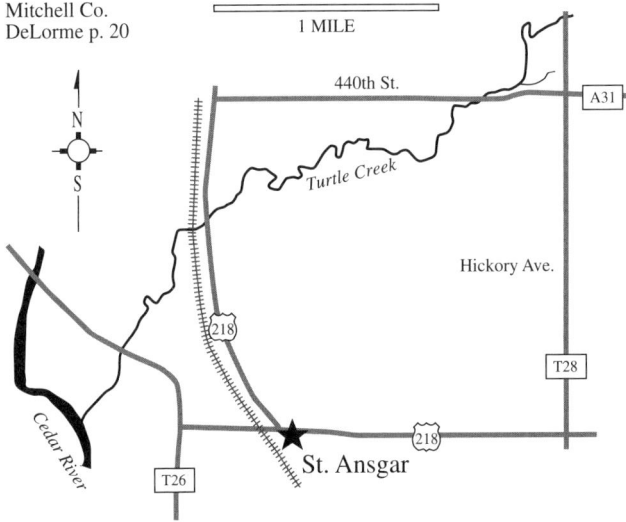

Turtle Creek
Mitchell Co.
DeLorme p. 20

Iowa Trout Streams

WAPSI (WAPSIPINICON) RIVER

The Wapsi is a good-size stream that you can find by taking A23 (470th Street) west out of the north side of the town of McIntire. You can fish near a fence crossing just west of town where a bridge crosses the stream; or, you can continue west, then turn north on Underwood Avenue to reach the upper end of the stocked section. The stream runs through a wildlife management area that bears the characteristics of prime pheasant-hunting ground.

The Trout Country Panhandle

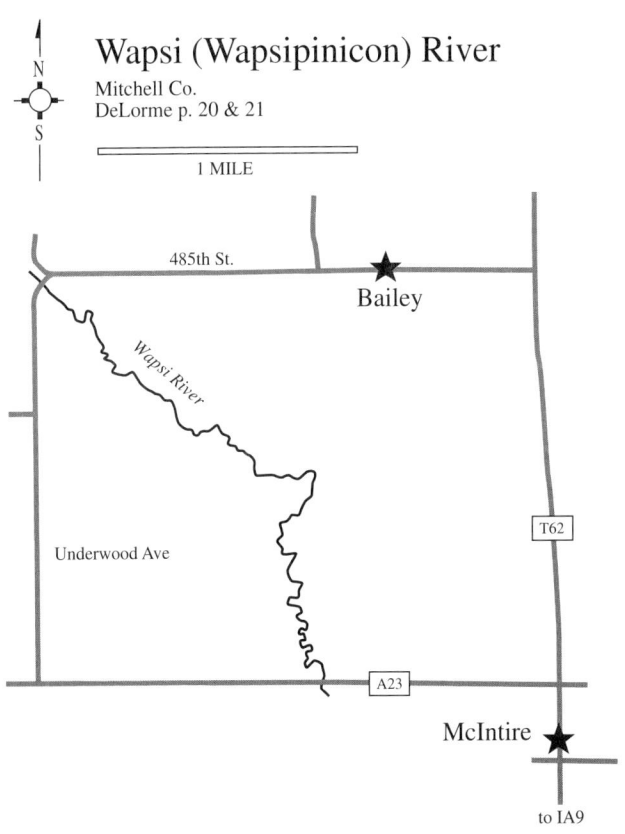

Wapsi (Wapsipinicon) River
Mitchell Co.
DeLorme p. 20 & 21

PART 3

REFLECTIONS

Good company.

Reflections

IN RETROSPECT

I arrived at this point in the text through a process that involved fishing, writing, fishing some more, drawing the maps, fishing some more, researching details, fishing some more, taking the photos, fishing some more, and so forth. In one month alone, I seriously fished 18 streams. In one four-day trip I visited every stream in the state, fishing many more streams in the process. During all of the "fishing some more" episodes, I noticed things that I want to emphasize here.

Without being conscious that I was doing it, whether I was driving or taking pictures or fishing, I spent each day in trout country deciding where I wanted to fish at dark. I was enjoying a particularly nice afternoon at Glovers, and as the sun started sinking I noticed I'd begun hurrying. Without it ever forming as a concrete thought, at some point during the day I had decided that at dark I wanted to be at the middle bridge on Otter Creek. Once there, I found and caught the best fish of the day.

Another thing I noticed was that my fly selection is geared toward streams that I fish regularly, such as Spring Branch and French Creek, which have healthy populations of aquatic insects. Not all streams do, and from now on I will carry more streamers and wooly worms with me—probably a whole box of them. They'll also work well on all streams during the early hours, before the morning hatches start coming off. In case you don't know it, I'll add here that there are monster browns in many of these streams that can only be caught after dark, usually on streamers.

Another thing I mentioned earlier that deserves reiteration is the importance of walking, especially on your first visit to a stream. For fly anglers, the upper reaches of the streams where the water is cleaner and quicker are often the best. If you can, resist the temptation to start fishing at the first fishable water you encounter.

In the preceding pages, I've tried to err on the side of optimism; while visiting new streams and revisiting familiar ones, I found that I'm more enthused than ever about Iowa trout fishing. I have a long list of new places where I want to spend some serious days fishing.

Not only are there lots of fish out there, there are some *big* fish out there. While walking one section of stream, rod under my arm, I saw an exceptionally nice brown feeding in the rocks. I was leisurely tying on a nymph to show to him when just 20 feet away, on the upstream side of a small rock, a two-foot brown porpoised so slowly and deliberately that I could count his spots. The memory is a little chilling,

Reflections

but I swear he looked me in the eye. By the time I changed to a different fly I had buck fever so badly I put my first backcast in the weeds, freed it, and then promptly put my first forward cast in some branches hanging out over the rock.

That doesn't usually happen to me anywhere, and is even less likely when I'm out West, where large fish are more common. The point is, try to be mentally prepared for large fish when you find them, which will be more often than you expect, yet not often enough to be commonplace.

Reflections

LOOSE ENDS

As you might imagine, during the concentrated fishing I did just before bringing this to print, I tied hundreds of knots. I realized then that they are too important to overlook in these pages. If you struggle with knots, they become costly in terms of lost fish and incurred frustration. Equally costly are the ones we don't tie when we should—the tippet that needs to be lengthened, the heavier tippet that we should use to turn over a larger fly, the fly that should be retied after catching a few fish, and the wind knots we ignore—simply because we are avoiding tying a knot.

There are only three knots you really need to know on the water, but the time that you need them most is right at dark with the wind hammering your face and your waders full of ice water. That's the time you'll break off your fly just as you spot a trophy fish rising. The knots you need, you need to tie swiftly and correctly without having to think.

If you have a permanent loop on your fly line and spend your evenings at home rebuilding used leaders so you'll always have one ready, the number of on-the-water knots drops to one, the improved clinch knot for tying on the fly.

There are always new knots to try, and although I'm handy with knots and learn new ones easily, the three I rely on most are ones I've used for years and years. The terminology in the following instructions has nautical roots—the "tag" end is the portion you will eventually trim away, and the "standing portion" is the part that remains attached to something.

Begin with an eye toward craftsmanship; speed will come with time. One of the most common mistakes I see is people not allowing enough tag end when they start a knot. Read the instructions. I have had people go out of their way to tell me that, after years of trying, they learned to tie the perfection loop by reading the instructions on the following pages.

Reflections

THE IMPROVED CLINCH KNOT

This is the old standby that most people already use for securing a hook.

STEPS IN TYING THE IMPROVED CLINCH KNOT:

1. Pass the end of tippet through the hook eye.

2. Wrap the tag end around the standing line 4 to 8 times, depending on the tippet diameter. (The lighter the tippet, the more wraps you'll need.)

3. Bring the tag end back through the loop nearest the hook eye.

4. Pass the tag end through the second loop formed in step 3. Moisten the knot as you tighten it. Pull the standing end until the knot is snug against the hook eye. Trim the tag as close to the knot as possible.

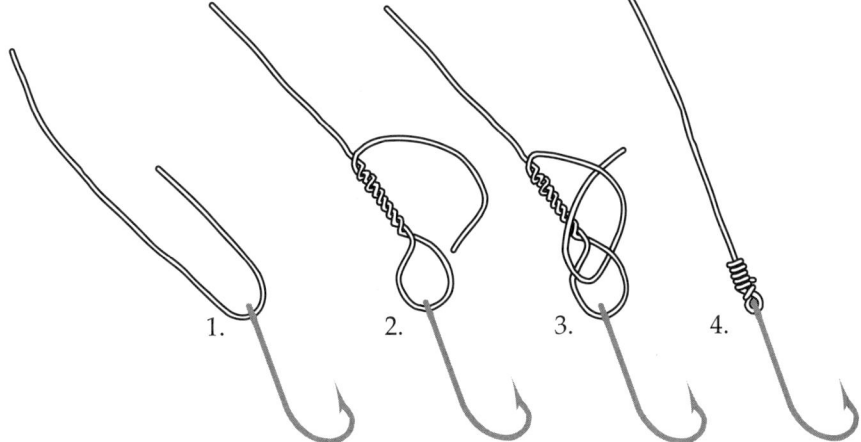

THE PERFECTION LOOP

This is the one knot for which I know of no acceptable substitute; I have never been satisfied with the results of the Surgeon's Loop. I use the Perfection Loop on the permanent leader butt that is attached to the fly line and on the butt of every leader. It's a "must learn" knot. Don't skimp on the amount you leave for the tag end. Start out by practicing it big and then gradually work smaller and smaller until you can tie a really small one.

STEPS IN TYING THE PERFECTION LOOP:

1. Form a loop in the leader by passing the tag end behind standing line, tag end facing right. (Hold it by pinching it between your thumb and forefinger where the lines cross. Leave tag end fairly long).

2. Form a second, smaller loop in front of the first by passing the tag end around and then behind the first loop. (You should now be pinching both loops.)

3. Pass the tag end between first two loops and hold it in place. (The tag end will be pointing left.)

4. Reach through the first loop from the back, grasp the second, smaller loop, and pull it backward through the first loop from behind.

5. Tighten the knot by pulling on the loop and standing line. When properly tied, the tag end will be at a right angle to the standing line and the loop will not slip. Trim the tag end closely.

Reflections

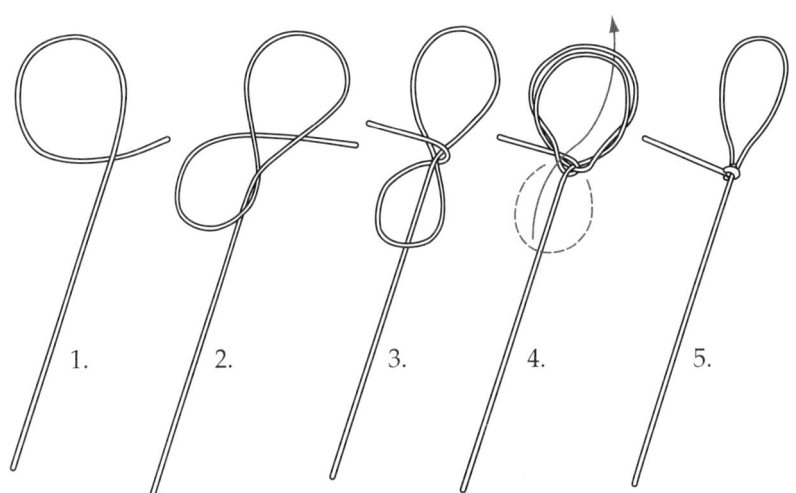

1. 2. 3. 4. 5.

THE DOUBLE SURGEON'S KNOT

This is the easiest knot for adding tippet, especially in low light or windy conditions. With practice, you can learn to tie this knot with your eyes closed. Though I use the traditional, and more complicated, Blood Knot for building leaders from scratch, this is the knot I use on the water.

STEPS IN TYING THE DOUBLE SURGEON'S KNOT:

1. Overlap the end of your leader and the new length of tippet you wish to add. The tag ends should point in opposite directions.

2. Treating the two lines as a single piece of mono, tie a loose overhand knot by passing the tag end of the leader and the standing end of the new tippet through the loop.

3. Pass the same ends through the loop a second time to form a double overhand knot.

4. Moisten the knot. Tighten by first pulling on all four ends, then by pulling just the standing ends. Trim the tag ends as closely as possible.

Iowa Trout Streams

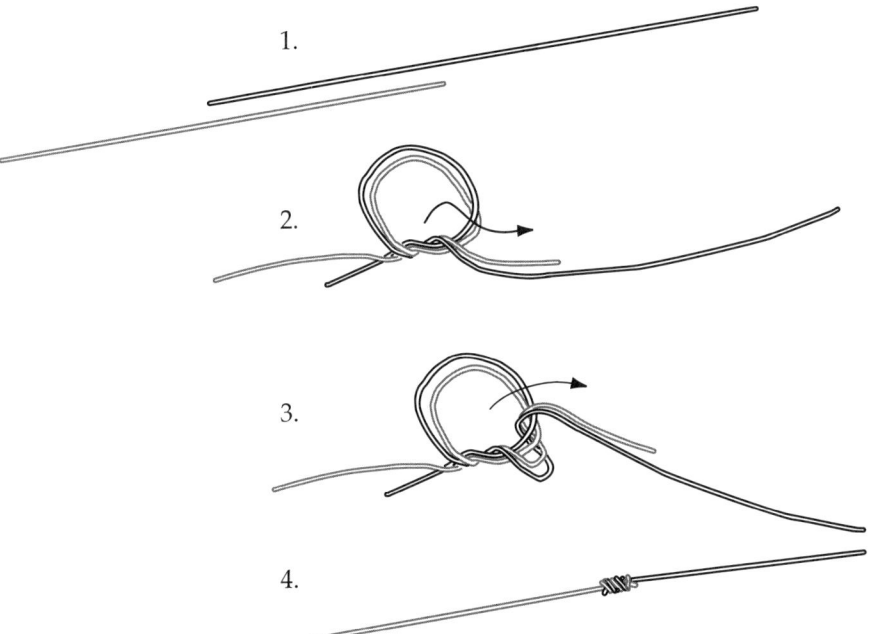

A Traveling Tip

It isn't a knot, but I include here a good tip for securing your fly and leader while you walk or drive around. By bringing the leader down under the reel seat and back up along the rod, you can hook the fly in any nearby snake guide. This allows you to leave an ample portion of the fly line itself outside the tip of the rod so it will be ready to use quickly when you start fishing again. When you try this you will see that if you need a little more slack because the fly is a little short of reaching the next guide, you just grab the line from the reel between any two snake guides and pull a little more from the reel, moving it toward the tip (the same direction you need to move the fly).

A Fable

Remember fables? Like "The Hare and the Tortoise" or "The Fox and the Crow"? Here is one I want to leave with you. I heard it told by a bartender to a tourist who was grumbling about the "fly-fishing only" restriction on the Railroad Ranch section of the Henry's Fork. That section of the river was passed on from railroad tycoon E. H. Harriman to his sons and eventually to the State of Idaho. Roland Harriman was the one who loved and managed the river. The complaining tourist couldn't understand why he wasn't allowed to at least use artificial lures with his spinning rod. The bartender explained it this way:

> For years Mister Harriman allowed everyone to fish on the river through his property, and for years Mister Harriman watched other fishermen trash the streamside while fly fishers came behind them and picked up the litter they'd left. So when he passed away, Mister Harriman left the ranch to the State of Idaho with the provision that it be posted 'fly-fishing only.'

Like I said, I pass the story along as a fable, undocumented but undisputed. I do know that since hearing it, I've gone a little farther out of my way to round up other people's empty containers and drink cans. As we hope and work to restore more streams and expand the populations of wild trout, our reputation as good outdoor citizens certainly won't hurt. Our previous efforts have been realized in the fine trout fishing that Iowa already has to offer.

Index of Streams

In Alphabetical Order

Bankston (Middle Fork, Little Maquoketa) 150
Bear Creek. 140
Bigalk Creek 120
Big Mill Creek. 156
Bloody Run 86
Bohemian Creek 122
Brush Creek. 161
Buck Creek 134
Clear Creek 124
Coldwater Creek 118
Coon Creek 110
Ensign Hollow 83
Fountain Springs 148
French Creek. 90, 102
Glovers Creek. 138
Grannis Creek 140
Hickory Creek. 128
Joy Springs 146
Little Mill Creek 159
Little Paint Creek 126
Little Turkey River 146
Maquoketa River 146
Mink Creek 142
North Bear Creek 98
North Cedar Creek. 130
Otter Creek 138
Paint Creek 126
Patterson Creek 113

185

Pine Creek 113
Richmond Springs 143
Silver Creek 113
Sny Magill 130
South Bear Creek 98
South Cedar Creek 136
South Pine Creek 89
Spring Branch Creek 77
Spring Creek 164
Swiss Valley 154
Trout Run 108
Trout River 110
Turkey River (Big Spring) 132
Turtle Creek 165
Twin Bridges 148
Twin Springs 109
Waterloo Creek 95
Wapsi (Wapsipinicon) River 166
West Canoe Creek 116
Wexford Creek 124

INDEX OF STREAMS

BY COUNTY

ALLAMAKEE COUNTY

Clear Creek 124
French Creek............................ 90, 102
Hickory Creek.............................. 128
Little Paint Creek 126
Paint Creek 126
Patterson Creek 113
Pine Creek 113
Silver Creek 113
Waterloo Creek 95
Wexford Creek.............................. 124

CLAYTON COUNTY

Bloody Run................................... 86
Buck Creek 134
Ensign Hollow 83
Joy Springs 146
Maquoketa River 146
North Cedar Creek 130
Sny Magill.................................. 130
South Cedar Creek 136
Turkey River (Big Spring) 132

DELAWARE COUNTY

Fountain Springs 148
Little Turkey River 146
Richmond Springs 143
Spring Branch Creek 77
Twin Bridges................................ 148

Dubuque County

Bankston 150
Swiss Valley 154

Fayette County

Bear Creek. 140
Glovers Creek 138
Grannis Creek 140
Mink Creek 142
Otter Creek 138

Howard County

Bigalk 120

Jackson County

Big Mill Creek. 156
Brush Creek. 161
Little Mill Creek 159

Mitchell County

Spring Creek. 164
Turtle Creek 165
Wapsi (Wapsipinicon) River 166

Winneshiek County

Bohemian Creek 122
Coldwater Creek 118
Coon Creek. 110
North Bear Creek 98
South Bear Creek 98
South Pine 89
Trout Run 108
Trout River 110
Twin Springs. 109
West Canoe Creek 116

Appendix

For information on Iowa's trout program or to schedule a tour of the facility, contact:

Manchester Trout Hatchery
22693 205th Avenue
Manchester, Iowa 52057
319-927-3276
Stocking information: 319-927-5736

Big Spring Rearing Station
16212 Big Spring Road
Elkader, Iowa 52043
319-245-2446
Stocking information: 319-245-1699

Decorah Rearing Station
2321 Siewers Spring Road
Decorah, Iowa 52101
319-382-8324
Stocking information: 319-382-3315

For general information, contact:

Iowa Department of Natural Resources
Wallace State Office Building
Des Moines, Iowa 50319-0034
515-281-5145 or 515-281-FISH
www.state.ia.us/fish

1-800-ASK-FISH

Iowa Trout Streams

For Information on Allamakee County:

Allamakee County Economic Development
& Tourism Commission
12 East Main
Waukon, Iowa 52172
319-568-2624
800-824-1424
www.visitiowa.com

For information on Winneshiek County:

Winneshiek County Tourism & Development
300 West Water Street
P.O. Box 288
Decorah, Iowa 52101
800-463-4092
www.decorah-iowa.com

For information on Fayette County:

Fayette County Tourism Council
P.O. Box 528
Fayette, Iowa 52124
319-425-4447
800-798-4447

For information on Clayton County:

Clayton County Development Group
132 South Main Street
P.O. Box 778
Elkader, Iowa 52043-0778
319-245-2201
800-488-7572
www.claytoncounty-iowa.com

Iowa Trout Streams

Iowa Division of Tourism:

Iowa Department of Economic Development
Division of Tourism
200 East Grand Avenue
Des Moines, Iowa 50309
515-242-4700
www.state.ia.us/tourism
info@ided.state.ia.us

Trout-Fishing Organizations:

Hawkeye Fly Fishers Association
P.O. Box 947
Iowa City, Iowa 52244
319-683-2864
www.commonlink.com/hffa

Federation of Fly Fishers
www.fedflyfish.org

Trout Unlimited
1500 Wilson Boulevard
Suite 310
Arlington, Virginia 22209-2404
Phone—703-522-0200
Fax—703-284-9400
www.tu.org

Jene & Kathy's Shop:

2nd Avenue Bait & Fly Shop II
133 Franklin Avenue
Des Moines, Iowa 50314
515-282-4217
www.iowaflyfishing.com